BUILDING THE SCIENCE DEPARTMENT

STORIES OF SUCCESS

BUILDING
— THE —
SCIENCE
DEPARTMENT

STORIES OF SUCCESS

WAYNE MELVILLE
DOUG JONES
TODD CAMPBELL

National Science Teachers Association
Arlington, Virginia

National Science Teachers Association

Claire Reinburg, Director
Rachel Ledbetter, Managing Editor
Deborah Siegel, Associate Editor
Amanda Van Beuren, Associate Editor
Donna Yudkin, Book Acquisitions Manager

ART AND DESIGN
Will Thomas Jr., Director
Joe Butera, Senior Graphic Designer, cover and
    interior design

PRINTING AND PRODUCTION
Catherine Lorrain, Director

NATIONAL SCIENCE TEACHERS ASSOCIATION
David L. Evans, Executive Director
David Beacom, Publisher

1840 Wilson Blvd., Arlington, VA 22201
www.nsta.org/store
For customer service inquiries, please call 800-277-5300.

NSTA is committed to publishing material that promotes the best in inquiry-based science education. However, conditions of actual use may vary, and the safety procedures and practices described in this book are intended to serve only as a guide. Additional precautionary measures may be required. NSTA and the authors do not warrant or represent that the procedures and practices in this book meet any safety code or standard of federal, state, or local regulations. NSTA and the authors disclaim any liability for personal injury or damage to property arising out of or relating to the use of this book, including any of the recommendations, instructions, or materials contained therein.

Cataloging-in-Publication Data are available from the Library of Congress.
ISBN: 978-1-68140-274-1
e-ISBN: 978-1-68140-275-8

SUSTAINABLE FORESTRY INITIATIVE   Certified Sourcing
www.sfiprogram.org
SFI-00756

CONTENTS

FOREWORD ix

ACKNOWLEDGMENTS...xiii

ABOUT THE AUTHORS xv

ABOUT OUR COLLEAGUES...xvii

1 Scientific Activity and Its Representation in the *Framework*, the *NGSS*, and Science Classrooms   1

Scientific Activity..1

Scientific Activity and the *NGSS* 3

Differences Between Current Classroom Experiences
and Those Supporting the *NGSS* 4

Vignette 1. Learning About Forces and Motion With
Ramps in the Middle School Life Science Classroom 6

Vignette 2. Explaining the Outbreak of Lyme Disease in
the Middle School Life Science Classroom...7

Conclusion 9

Summary 10

Questions to Consider..10

2 Learning to Change in the Department   11

Difficult to Change: Understanding Present Practice 12

Professional Learning 15

The Importance of the Science Department 17

Leadership 19

Conclusion 21

Summary 21

Questions to Consider..22

3 Building the Conditions for Learning — 25

A Framework for Professional Learning 27

The Professional Learning Context 28

The Content of Professional Learning 30

Activities That Promote Professional Learning 33

Learning Processes 35

Conclusion 36

Summary 37

Questions to Consider 38

4 The Professional Learning Context — 39

Is This Guy for Real? (Shawn) 39

Building a Team of Science Teachers (Liz).. 42

We're Talking About How Science Is Done (Mike). 44

Modify It and Risk It All Again (Steve)... 46

The Right People on the Bus (Julie) 47

Commentary on the Professional Learning Context 50

Conclusion 57

Summary 58

Questions to Consider 58

5 The Content of Professional Learning — 61

A "Student of Science and of Education" (Shawn)...............................62

Experience the Material (Liz) 64

This Looks Very Different for Me Today (Mike) 66

I'm a Bit of a Dinosaur, but I've Learned (Steve). 68

An Appreciation of Both Real Science *and* Real Teaching (Julie)....................... 69

Commentary on the Content of Professional Learning......................................72

Conclusion 79

Summary 80

Questions to Consider...81

6 The Activities That Promote Professional Learning 83

I Can Foster Knowledge, Inquiry, and Creativity (Shawn) 84

We Started Moving Away From Direct Instruction (Liz) 86

They Are Teaching Me (Mike) 88

I Spent a Lot of Time in the Literature (Steve) 91

We See Opportunities to Grow Professionally (Julie) 92

Commentary on Activities That Promote Professional Learning 94

Conclusion 102

Summary 103

Questions to Consider...104

7 The Learning Processes That Teachers Engage In 105

And Yes, I Am Guilty of That, Too (Shawn) 106

There Became Some Natural Dissonance (Liz)...108

Breaking Down What I Knew (Mike)... 111

Again, That's Science (Steve) 112

How Can We Investigate Change? (Julie) 113

Commentary on the Learning Processes That Teachers Engage In 115

Conclusion 119

Summary 120

Questions to Consider...121

8 And Now the Work Begins ...   **123**

Supporting the Changing Needs of Teachers 124

The Role of the Teacher Leader...125

Science Leadership Content Knowledge..126

Intangibles 127

Where to Next? 128

Resources..128

Summary 129

Questions to Consider..130

REFERENCES 133

APPENDIX: The Components of Professional Learning
and Their Constituent Areas...137

INDEX..143

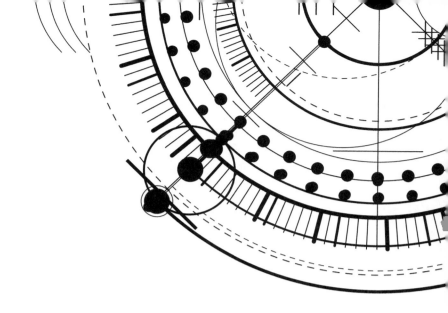

Foreword

Stories. Teachers love to tell stories of their classrooms and their practices. The stories can be about their successes, their difficulties, their triumphs, and their disasters. They can be inspiring and they can be harrowing. They can also instruct, guide, and help us learn.

In our early thinking about this book, we decided that we wanted to work with the stories of teachers who had negotiated—and continue to negotiate—the (at times) perilous paths of reform. What were their stories, and what could we, as a larger audience, learn from them? What were the contexts that supported their learning? What did they need to know, learn, and understand as they looked to challenge their practices? What activities did they engage in that helped them change their classrooms? And what were the processes by which they came to begin to understand the lofty ambitions of reform documents in terms of their own classrooms and departments? These are all important questions, as the work of teachers is at the heart of any and all reform efforts.

We were also interested in the stories of teachers at different stages in their careers, for we know that the professional learning needs of teachers are constantly evolving. The stories that new teachers tell are necessarily different from the stories told by teachers with many years of experience. The stories told by teachers who take on leadership roles, either formally as department chairs or informally as teacher leaders, are different again from those teachers who are more focused on their classrooms. Regardless of experience or leadership role, the work of becoming a teacher never ends, so we suspected that there may be some common themes running throughout the teachers' stories, regardless of career stage.

In planning to ask teachers to write of their teaching and learning, we were aware that just asking somebody to write on such an open-ended topic was bound to be met with the question "Where do I start?" Clearly we needed a framework that would provide a guide for the stories to be told but not restrict what was important to the story writer. To this end, we used the framework developed by Helen Timperley, Aaron Wilson, Heather Barrar, and Irene Fung and published in New Zealand in 2007 (available from *www.oecd.org/edu/school/48727127.pdf*).

Synthesizing research into the professional learning of teachers, the framework developed four basic components of effective professional learning opportunities for teachers:

1. Professional learning context

2. Content of the professional learning opportunities

3. Activities that promote professional learning

4. Learning processes that teachers engage in

For each of these components of professional learning, the framework identifies specific constituent areas that can have a positive impact on student learning in science. The full framework is shown in the appendix (p. 137).

Having a framework to guide writing is one thing—having teachers to work within that framework and tell their stories is quite another. To bring the framework to life, we decided to approach teachers with whom we had worked and who were committed to reforming their teaching and learning or who came to our attention by the contributions they were making to science education, both in their own schools and further afield. The teachers who agreed to work with us have taught from 4 years to more than 28 years in secondary schools in Canada and the United States. Some have worked as department chairs, and all are teacher leaders in some capacity. All are exemplary teachers committed to both their students and our profession. Working with Jason, Shawn, Liz, Mike, Steve, and Julie has been a privilege for us, and we are indebted to them for their candor and their ongoing contributions to teaching and learning. We trust that you will find their stories as insightful as we found them.

This book can be seen as comprising two parts—the first sets out an understanding of scientific activity (one of the key tenets of the current reforms in science education in North America), the rationale for concentrating on the department as a place for building and sustaining teacher professional learning, and the aforementioned professional learning framework. In Chapter 1, we begin by outlining how scientific activity can be used to frame professional learning within science departments on the grounds that one of the major roles of the science department is to accurately represent the discipline for *all of our students*. It should be noted that Chapter 1 connects the accurate representation of the discipline to the *Next Generation Science Standards* (*NGSS*). In addition, it should be noted that the *NGSS* were developed from *A Framework for K–12 Science Education* (referred to as the *Framework*). This is an essential compendium document necessary for understanding the rationale, organization, and commitments of the *NGSS*. Although not all U.S. states have adopted the *NGSS*, most have aligned their new state standards with the *Framework.* In Chapter 1, we assume that the reader has some familiarity with the *NGSS,* the *Framework,* and three-dimensional learning as the cornerstone of these documents. If you are not familiar with these documents, we recommend referring to some of the following introductory resources for supporting a beginning understanding of these foundational documents:

- "Three-Dimensional Instruction: Using a New Type of Teaching in the Science Classroom" (available from *http://static.nsta.org/files/tst1508_50.pdf*)

- "Next Generation Science Standards: What's Different, and Do They Matter?" (available from *http://stemteachingtools.org/brief/14*)

- STEM Teaching Tools (available from *http://stemteachingtools.org*)

Chapter 2 provides an understanding of the science department as it currently exists in secondary schools and the powerful influence that it has on teaching, learning, and professional development. Chapter 3 details the professional learning framework developed by Timperley et al. (2007), thus setting the stage for the second section of the book—the teachers' stories.

The second part, starting with Chapter 4, is structured so that we work through each of the components of the professional learning framework (context, content, activities, and processes) through the stories (hereafter called *vignettes*) told by our colleagues. Each chapter starts with Jason providing a brief overview of his experiences before Shawn, Liz, Mike, Steve, and Julie take turns discussing their thoughts on professional learning within the framework. The arrangement here is deliberate; the vignettes are arranged in order of experience, from beginning teacher to more experienced teachers. Following the vignettes is a commentary that highlights the key points and implications for teacher learning that emerge from the work of our colleagues. An important feature of our previous book, *Reimagining the Science Department* (NSTA Press, 2015), that we have included in this book are questions to ask yourself as both a science teacher and a teacher leader. Such questions are important because to challenge our own stories is to start to make changes that improve our practices and start to bring those practices into greater alignment with the ideals of the current reform documents.

As you start looking at and learning from the stories of other teachers, please remember to contact us if there is any way we can help you in your work.

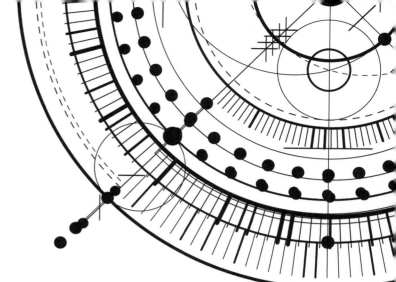

Acknowledgments

There are several people we need to thank for helping bring this book to life. First and foremost, we must acknowledge the work of our colleagues Jason Pilot, Shawn Devin, Liz Potter-Nelson, Mike Sewards, Steve Lankin, and Julie Gaubatz. It is always a privilege to work with such talented professionals. Without them, there would be no book.

Thanks to Claire Reinburg, Rachel Ledbetter, and Donna Yudkin at NSTA Press for their ongoing support, advice, and encouragement.

Thank you to our colleagues who critiqued early drafts of our work—Jeremy Peacock, Matt Roy, and Aaron Stephens—for making the end result far better than it would otherwise have been. We would also be remiss if we did not thank our NSTA reviewers for their contributions in improving the quality of our work.

Finally, to Rosemary, Lisa, and Joy, our significant others, for always being there and keeping us grounded.

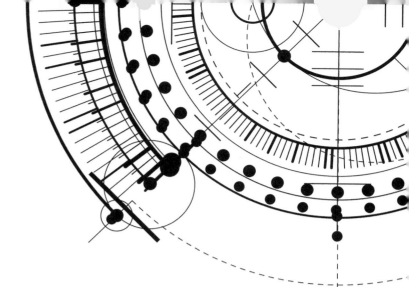

About the Authors

Wayne Melville is a professor of science education and assistant dean at Lakehead University in Thunder Bay, Ontario, Canada. He taught secondary science in Australia from 1989 to 2005, eventually becoming a department chair. During his school teaching career, he completed a master's of science and a doctorate in science education and was a national finalist for a science teaching award organized by the Australian Academy of Science. Since moving to Lakehead University in Ontario, Canada, he has published more than 70 articles in the field of science education. He has been a committed member of the National Science Teachers Association (NSTA) for many years and contributes to NSTA journals and conferences. His e-mail address is *wmelvill@lakeheadu.ca*.

Doug Jones is a science faculty member at Sir Winston Churchill Collegiate and Vocational Institute in Thunder Bay, Ontario, Canada. He has served as a science chair for 20 years of his 34-year career. Doug has taught in the Lakehead University department of education for several years and has developed several courses in science education. Doug and his department are well known in science education circles for their paradigm-shifting work in the teaching and learning of secondary science, along with significant work regarding scientific literacy, professional learning communities, assessment and evaluation, and growing one's personal professional practice. The department has also mentored more than 150 preservice teachers over the past 20 years. Doug enjoys the research and writing relationship he has with Wayne and Todd and is proud to be a contributing member of both the Science Teachers' Association of Ontario and NSTA. His e-mail address is *dougyjones@gmail.com*.

Todd Campbell is a faculty member in the Neag School of Education at the University of Connecticut. His research focuses on cultivating imaginative and equitable representations of STEM activity. This is accomplished in formal science learning environments through partnering with preservice and in-service science teachers and leaders to collaboratively focus on supporting student use of modeling as an anchoring epistemic practice to reason about events that happen in the natural world. This work extends into informal learning environments through a focus on the iterative design of informal learning spaces and equity-focused STEM identity research. Todd is a former high school and middle school science teacher and is a proud member of NSTA. He consistently contributes to NSTA journals as an author and reviewer. His e-mail address is *todd.campbell@uconn.edu*.

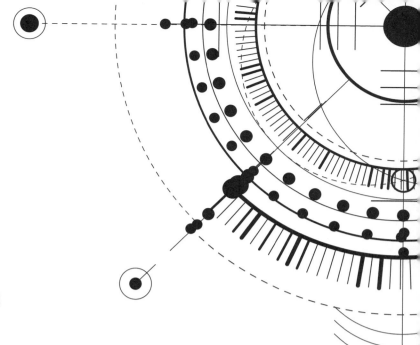

About Our Colleagues

This book would not have been possible without the thoughtful contributions of our colleagues, who have written of their experiences in science education.

Jason Pilot is currently the head of science at Sir Winston Churchill Collegiate and Vocational Institute in Thunder Bay, Ontario, Canada. He has taught general science, chemistry, and environmental science for 14 years. He also taught grades 4 and 5 for one year and spent two years as a secondary resource teacher for Lakehead Public Schools. As a teacher, he is always trying to bring real-world activities into the classroom, which has driven his development of problem-based learning and inquiry.

Shawn Devin is a secondary school science teacher in the Toronto Catholic District School Board. As a young and passionate teacher, now in his fourth year, he strives to foster an exciting and engaging learning environment that uses investigatory activities, cool experiments, differentiated teaching strategies, social learning, and real-life connections. He was fortunate to be awarded the Don Galbraith Preservice Teacher Award of Excellence from the Science Teachers' Association of Ontario in 2012.

Elizabeth (Liz) Potter-Nelson is a science teacher at Stevens Point Area Senior High School in Wisconsin and has taught for 11 years. Before recently returning to the classroom, she spent five years as a department chair working closely with teachers to transition their curriculum to be phenomena-driven and aligned with the *Next Generation Science Standards* (*NGSS*).

For more than 28 years, **Mike Sewards** has been a teacher of exercise physiology, general science, and chemistry in Thunder Bay, Ontario, Canada. He has been recognized provincially as producing classroom environments that encourage powerful learning and has worked on a number of Ontario Ministry of Education projects in this area. He has also nurtured many preservice teachers and has been an active member of his school's professional development team.

Steve Lankin is a chemistry and physics teacher in Thunder Bay, Ontario, Canada. Some say that he can make his subjects come alive for students with a combination of brilliant teaching strategies and humor. He believes that knowing what science should look like—in both classrooms and real-world scenarios—is fundamental to working with students, preservice teachers, and other teachers. He has taught for 18 years.

Julie Gaubatz, EdD, teaches science and chairs the science department at Hinsdale South High School in Darien, Illinois. With more than 20 years of teaching experience coupled with a background in laboratory research, she is particularly interested in models of change, inquiry, and leadership that improve students' experiences in secondary science education.

Finally, before we begin, we need to highlight an important point. Many of the teachers we have worked with have been involved in reforming their practices for many years. This means that many of the vignettes reference work that supports the teaching of science as inquiry as is emphasized in the *National Science Education Standards* (NRC 1996). Although the terminology has changed (see Bybee 2011 for a concise explanation), the importance of the vignettes lies in their power to reveal how teachers have gone about the work of change, which is necessary with *A Framework for K–12 Science Education* and the *NGSS*. When our colleagues talk about "inquiry," rest assured that they are talking of evolving practices that align with the latest reform documents.

Scientific Activity and Its Representation in the *Framework*, the *NGSS*, and Science Classrooms

Although it can be argued that there are many important reasons for focusing on building the science department, no reason is more important than the role of the science department in accurately representing the discipline for all of our students. This entails considering not only how to represent the central ideas of the different science disciplines (e.g., physics, biology, Earth science) but also representing how explanations are constructed and critiqued within these science disciplines. Therefore, as a foundation for this book, we begin by outlining how scientific activity can be used to frame the work within science departments and how it aligns with contemporary visions of science teaching and learning. Throughout Western nations, these visions share a common dual emphasis "on students' understanding how science works—the nature of science and its processes—as well as the content of science" (Tytler 2007, p. 23). Within the United States, the vision is clearly outlined in both *A Framework for K–12 Science Education* (the *Framework;* NRC 2012) and the *Next Generation Science Standards* (*NGSS;* NGSS Lead States 2013). This initial framing is then followed by some discussion about the difficulties that teachers have historically experienced in challenging and changing their pedagogical practices. Finally, the chapter ends with a "road map" describing how this book helps address these historical difficulties from the perspectives of teachers at different stages in their careers as well as professional learning that has been of assistance to them.

Scientific Activity

Scientific activity can be understood as the activities that scientists engage in during their day-to-day work. Much of our understanding of the day-to-day work of scientists comes from science studies researchers who have observed scientists engaging in their work over prolonged periods of time. One outcome of this research into

Scientific Activity and Its Representation in the *Framework*, the *NGSS*, and Science Classrooms

science studies that has greatly influenced science education—and our attempts to represent scientific activity for students in classrooms—can be seen in the inclusion of *developing and using models* as well as the other science and engineering practices in the *Framework* and the *NGSS*. Modeling has been highlighted in the *Framework* and the *NGSS* because science studies researchers such as Nersessian (1999) and Giere (2004) identified how the primary work of scientists lies in the construction, revision, and testing of hypothetical models.

In thinking about scientific activity, the use of the word *activity* here is intentional because it finds its roots in activity theory, which is essentially concerned with understanding human activity (Vygotsky 1978). In activity theory, three primary constructs for thinking about human pursuits, or the reason for engaging in activity, are foregrounded: the *subjects* (or those involved in activity), the *objects* (or the motivations the subjects have for engaging in activity), and the *tools* (or the resources that are used to work toward achieving the motivations or object of activity; see Figure 1.1 for a representation of how subjects, tools, and objects interact in activity; Luria 1976; Vygotsky 1987).

When the activity theory lens is applied to the work of scientists who are engaged

FIGURE 1.1. **Activity Theory**

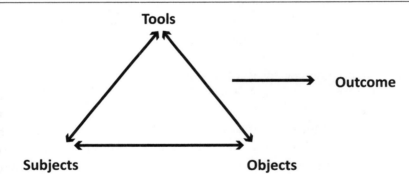

in scientific activity, the *subjects* are the scientists and the *objects* (or motivations) of their pursuits are explaining phenomena or solving problems. Further, *tools* are anything that helps scientists achieve their pursuit. An example of this can be seen in Darwin's work to explain the varying beak sizes of the Galapagos finch populations found on isolated islands throughout the Galapagos Islands. A simplistic depiction of Darwin's work represented as scientific activity would suggest that Darwin (the *subject*) used science practices such as observations and evidence collection, along with his proposed idea of natural selection (all *tools*), to explain the varied beak sizes of the Galapagos finches (the *object*).[1] Here, Darwin, and subsequently others, could also further apply the tools of natural selection and other science practices to explain similar phenomena found as a result of the isolated nature of populations of species throughout the Galapagos Islands (e.g., the varied Galapagos giant tortoises' shell sizes and shapes). As a result, natural selection can be applied as a tool to explain a wide range of naturally occurring phenomena far beyond the Galapagos Islands.

Scientific Activity and the *NGSS*

As the activity theory lens is turned toward science classrooms, with an aim of representing scientific activity for all students, a clarified vision of the three dimensions of the *Framework* and the *NGSS* is found. In this, three-dimensional learning is defined as engaging students (*subjects*) in science and engineering practices (Dimension 1—*tools*) to use disciplinary crosscutting concepts (Dimension 2—*tools*) and core ideas (Dimension 3—*tools*) to explain phenomena or solve problems (*objects;* Krajcik 2015). An example of three-dimensional learning framed in terms of representations of scientific activity can be found by using the imploding tanker car example (*www.youtube.com/watch?v=Zz95_VvTxZM*) in Appendix D of the *NGSS* as Case Study 1. In this example, the entire unit is framed around students working over the course of several days to explain the imploding tanker car phenomenon. This example reveals how students move from their initial explanations of the phenomenon, which are more reliant on everyday ways of communicating and thinking, to more sophisticated explanations undergirded with more scientifically accepted ideas, supported by collected evidence at the end of the instructional unit. In this example, the teacher supports students in iteratively developing and using models across the unit, planning and carrying out investigations, engaging in argument from evidence, and constructing explanations as students' ideas are shared and differences are found across students' models. Beyond the science and engineering practices that students (*subjects*) use, the teacher also encourages students to draw on what they know about the particulate nature of matter in terms of how molecules interact and react to changes in temperature in the imploding tanker car. In this example, disciplinary core ideas such as HS-PS-1, "Matter and Its Interactions," are also used as *tools* to explain the imploding tanker car (*object*). In addition, although this is not as explicit in the example chronicled in the Appendix D *NGSS* case study, students could use crosscutting concepts (*tools*) such as "Energy

---

1   It is recognized here that Darwin and other scientists' work (e.g., theoretical physicists) could also be accurately characterized as undertaken with the aim of developing theory. This is not foregrounded here because the *Framework* and the *NGSS* writers have highlighted explaining phenomena and solving problems as necessary central pursuits in science classrooms in an effort to move away from a traditional focus on "learning about" theories and ideas toward a central focus on "figuring out" in the context of explaining phenomena or solving problems.

and Matter," "Cause and Effect," or "Systems and System Models" to aid in their attempts to explain the phenomena (*objects*) that have grounded the instructional unit. What is noteworthy in this example is that students in the representation of scientific activity have been positioned to see what they are doing across the unit as a human pursuit that aligns with those kinds of pursuits that drive scientific activity (i.e., constructing and critiquing explanations of events that happen in the world). In addition, to work on problems students are having with knowing, they pick up tools like modeling (science and engineering practice), ideas about the particulate nature of matter (disciplinary core idea), and cause and effect (crosscutting concept) in the context of three-dimensional learning to work toward accomplishing the aim of their pursuit: explaining phenomena. Although examples of three-dimensional learning can be found, and more and more will emerge as a result of the collective and synergistic efforts of teachers nationally, this type of science teaching and learning whereby "figuring out" is prioritized over "learning about" the products of "other people's science" is quite different from what is found in most science classrooms (NRC 2015), a point that will be taken up next. But first, Figures 1.2 and 1.3 portray the connections among activity theory represented in Figure 1.1., scientific activity (Figure 1.2), and classroom representations of scientific activity (Figure 1.3) to summarize how—and why—this book has been framed as an exploration of how science departments can support the work of teachers in representing scientific activity for their students.

Differences Between Current Classroom Experiences and Those Supporting the *NGSS*

National large-scale studies of U.S. classrooms reveal how many of the classroom experiences of students in science are not aligned with visions of science teaching and learning outlined in the *NGSS*. More specifically, national studies have revealed a lack of intellectual engagement, curricular activities in place of adequate sense making, and a failure to take students' prior knowledge into account or to seek evidence-based explanations (Banilower et al. 2013). Here, *sense making* is defined as "working on and with ideas—both students' ideas (including experiences, language, and ways of knowing) and authoritative ideas in texts and other materials—in ways that help generate meaningful connections" (Campbell, Schwarz, and Windschitl 2016, p. 69). Vignette 1 represents a depiction of some of the more traditional experiences that students have, and continue to experience, in classrooms throughout the United States.

FIGURE 1.2. **Scientific Activity Theory**

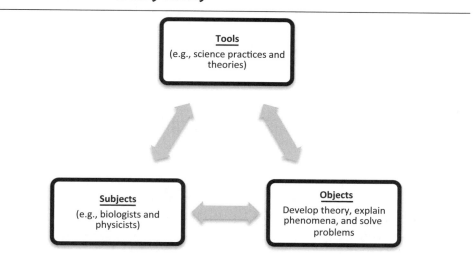

FIGURE 1.3. **Classroom Representations of Scientific Activity Theory**

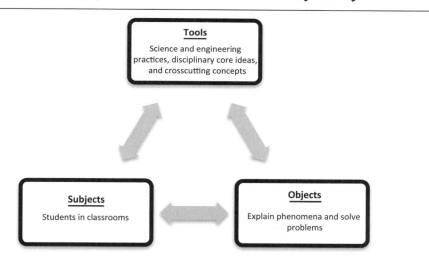

The vignettes found throughout the book, along with the questions at the end of each chapter, are, we believe, at the heart of the professional learning that can be supported by this book. This is especially true because these vignettes offer a glimpse into the classrooms of others, whereas the questions at the end of each chapter serve as reflective tools to support teachers and teacher leaders in building their science departments.

VIGNETTE 1

Learning About Forces and Motion With Ramps in the Middle School Life Science Classroom

Ms. Zaruba's first-period eighth-grade class in Utah has been learning about forces and motion. To start the unit, the students were introduced to the important vocabulary they would be learning about during this unit of instruction. This was accomplished initially as they completed a homework assignment in which they were given a list of important vocabulary words and asked to identify a definition for each. For example, students were asked to define force. Upon returning to class with their completed worksheets, the class reviewed the definitions the students had found and, with Ms. Zaruba's help, agreed on the most appropriate definitions for each vocabulary word. For example, when they discussed force, the students shared how most of their definitions described force as something that caused an object with mass to accelerate and how this could be described with the formula force = mass × acceleration ($F = ma$). Ms. Zaruba explained that this was an important initial step in learning about forces and motion because it was important that all the students know exactly what they were referring to as

they used these scientific words and ideas. Once Ms. Zaruba felt that the students had a common language, she engaged them in a laboratory exercise so that the students could see how the definition of force they arrived at (i.e., $F = ma$) could be used to predict how much relative force would be needed to pull a 50-gram weight up a wooden ramp compared with the amount of force it would take to pull a 100-gram weight up the same wooden ramp at an identical angle. By engaging in the laboratory with the step-by-step directions Ms. Zaruba provided, students were able to first predict that it would take more force to pull the 100-gram mass up the ramp compared with the 50-gram mass. And, upon measuring the force required to move the different masses up the ramp using a spring scale, they were able to confirm that more force was required to move the 100-gram mass. As part of the force and motion unit, students learned additional terms (e.g., acceleration) and were engaged in further laboratory exercises so that they could get a sense of the usefulness and accuracy of the ideas they were learning about.

In this vignette, students are focused on learning important science concepts. However, they are not engaged in science and engineering practices to accomplish a sensemaking pursuit (i.e., explain a phenomenon or solve a problem) in ways that might offer them insight into scientific activity. Instead, the ramps at different angles are used to demonstrate the validity of the science concepts, or the relationship between force, mass, and acceleration already revealed as the "settled science" they needed to learn. By not being faced with some uncertainty or struggle, students aren't really positioned to use science and engineering practices to work at knowing something. In addition, because the students started the unit learning vocabulary instead of initially sharing their own ideas and experiences with ramps in their everyday lives, they are not positioned to connect what they are learning in the science classroom with their everyday ways of thinking and knowing. If students aren't supported in reaching for science and engineering practices and scientific ideas when they encounter problems or the need to explain something in the classroom as they are introduced to these scientific ideas and practices, they likely won't see the value of these tools and begin to reach for them in their everyday lives in the future inside or outside of school. In fact, for most students, this type of experience that is still prevalent in many classrooms throughout the United States focuses more on the products of "other people's science" rather than something students would describe as "their own science" that is relevant to them.

If we were to move beyond doing "other people's science," what would that look like? Vignette 2 about Mr. Howard's class provides some insight into what a reformed classroom might look like for teachers and their students.

VIGNETTE 2

Explaining the Outbreak of Lyme Disease in the Middle School Life Science Classroom

Mr. Howard, a seventh-grade teacher in Connecticut, began a unit focused on the interdependent relationships found in ecosystems. In planning for this unit, Mr. Howard collaborated with another teacher in his department to identify an anchoring phenomenon that could serve as the reason students were engaging in the entire unit. In identifying the phenomenon, Mr. Howard and his colleague were committed to identifying a phenomenon that was complex enough to require students to coordinate several ideas to explain. The phenomenon that was selected was the increase in cases of Lyme disease reported in the United States since the 1980s. To begin the unit, Mr. Howard shared two graphs. One was a bar graph of Lyme disease cases in the United States from 1982 to 2008; the other was a graphical representation of where in the United States Lyme disease is found by county. In groups of two to three, students were asked to think about possible explanations for the increase in cases of Lyme disease they saw on the graphs over time. Given the history of Lyme disease in Connecticut, a few students suggested early on that ticks could be responsible for the spread of Lyme disease. After a short whole-class discussion during which students shared additional ideas, the class came to an initial consensus that ticks play an important role in the occurrence of

Lyme disease. At this point in the lesson, Mr. Howard asked the students to develop a *model* (i.e., a set of ideas for explaining something that happens in the world) to help refine their initial ideas about the increased cases of Lyme disease. After students were given time to create their initial models, each group shared their models with peers; this included the reasoning and evidence they thought were important for supporting their initial ideas. After the students shared and critiqued their initial models, Mr. Howard introduced a video that explained how malaria spreads between people by mosquitoes. In introducing the video, Mr. Howard shared how he thought the video might provide some ideas that could be useful in explaining the roles and mechanism by which ticks spread Lyme disease and other factors that might, over time, lead to an increase in this spread. In addition to the malaria video, Mr. Howard provided some selected articles for the class to read that described the relationship between ticks and deer. After the students had more ideas about how vectors spread disease (e.g., malaria) and information about how deer are also involved in the spread of Lyme disease, they were then asked to return to their initial models to revise them and again share them as a class. Then they could continue to work on a class consensus model to develop an evidence-based explanation of the increased cases of Lyme disease in the United States since the 1980s.

In contrast to Ms. Zaruba's classroom, Mr. Howard's class starts with a phenomenon for students to explain rather than vocabulary to learn. In addition, throughout the unit, students were positioned to share—and use—the ideas introduced by their peers or by Mr. Howard. When they engaged collaboratively in small groups or with the whole class to construct explanations, they were also concurrently engaged in the science and engineering practices of developing and using models and argument from evidence, among other practices, to make sense of the event that had happened in the world (i.e., the increased spread of Lyme disease). In Mr. Howard's classroom, in contrast to Ms. Zaruba's, students' ideas were important resources that were elicited and built on throughout the unit. Also, as important ideas were introduced in the pursuit of explaining the spread of Lyme disease, students were positioned to use them flexibly in the context of the evidence they were able to uncover in the originally introduced graphs. In the end, Mr. Howard's classroom provides a different approach to science teaching and learning that, similar to the imploding tanker car unit highlighted in Appendix D of the *NGSS* as Case Study 1 referenced earlier, involves students in sense making as they develop and use models, engage in argument from evidence, and construct explanations, among other practices, throughout the course of a unit of instruction.

Conclusion

Chapter 1 has focused on developing a clearer picture of scientific activity and what approximations of scientific activity might look like in classrooms. It is clear from large-scale national studies that experiences like those depicted in Appendix D of the *NGSS* as Case Study 1 and the vignette from Mr. Howard's classroom represent experiences that are historically different from those of most students in U.S. classrooms. Using the range of tools and resources (e.g., classroom video examples and planning heuristics) like those available from websites such as Ambitious Science Teaching (*www.ambitiousscienceteaching.org*) allows teachers to begin to reshape their students' classroom experiences so that they more authentically approximate scientific activity. Following on from our first book, *Reimagining the Science Department* (NSTA Press, 2015), the purpose of this book is to help science teachers working in science departments build spaces where this type of work is taken up and supported.

The *Framework* and the *NGSS* astutely recognize the important role of the entire educational system in shaping teaching and learning. They have pointed out how both the National Science Education Standards ("the Standards") and the push for approximating scientific activity in classrooms must permeate the educational system for the reformed vision of science education to be realized. This means that plans for implementing the Standards must include consideration of how they will guide curriculum, instruction, professional development, and student assessment (NRC 2012). What is evident here is that one teacher cannot achieve the visions of the *Framework* and the *NGSS* in isolation because much of the pressure on teachers often arises at different levels within the system (e.g., at the school or department level). Given this, we believe that the department represents one of the most important levels within the system whereby change and support can, and should, emerge. In this, as will be depicted throughout the remainder of the book, the department can become the space whereby professional learning is supported and policy is negotiated so that the visions of science teaching and learning outlined in the *Framework* and the *NGSS* are realized. What we present in the coming chapters is how those at different places in their careers (e.g., early-career teacher, veteran teacher, department chair) and in different contexts have begun (and continue) to make changes within their departments that have moved them toward realizing the reformed visions of the *Framework* and the *NGSS*. In addition, we have synthesized what we see as commonalities and differences across these contexts and offer advice for those considering initiating similar pursuits in their own departments. Before we get to our colleagues' stories, however, in Chapter 2 we set the stage for building the science department as a place conducive for professional learning by helping contextualize the work of science departments in their historical contexts

and by examining their importance in the current climate within which we find
ourselves.

Summary

- Although it can be argued that there are many important reasons for
  focusing on building the science department, no reason is more important
  than the role of the science department in accurately representing the
  discipline for—and to—all students.

- Scientific activity can be understood as the activities that scientists engage in
  day to day in their work (constructing and critiquing explanations of events
  that happen in the world).

- Three-dimensional learning can be characterized as a classroom version of
  scientific activity because it is defined as engaging students in science and
  engineering practices to use disciplinary crosscutting concepts and core
  ideas to explain phenomena or solve problems.

Questions to Consider

1. To what extent do you feel that representing the discipline of science to
   students is central to the work of your science department? What are
   possible strategies for making sure that this representation remains the
   central focus of departmental work?

2. What other historical examples of scientific activity can you articulate that
   might provide additional insight into scientific activity for your colleagues
   within your department and with your students?

3. What are ways you can ensure that students begin to see the work they are
   doing in classrooms within the department as representations of scientific
   activity? (*Note:* See the National Science Teachers Association Blog post
   from Cindy Passmore titled "Implementing the Next Generation Science
   Standards: How Your Classroom Is Framed Is as Important as What You
   Do in It" at *http://nstacommunities.org/blog/2014/11/10/implementing-the-next-
   generation-science-standards-how-your-classroom-is-framed-is-as-important-as-
   what-you-do-in-it* as a resource for thinking about this.)

Learning to Change in the Department

For the past 50 years, there have been consistent calls for teachers to engage students in more authentic representations of science in classrooms. This engagement is important to help students develop a sense of the practices that scientists use to develop strong knowledge claims, explain phenomena, and solve problems. School science is not alone in calling for reforms; math teachers have experienced the "math wars," history teachers are regularly challenged as to whose history should be taught, and all teachers are regularly challenged to be more interdisciplinary.

Although the core tenets of the disciplines remain relatively constant, there are ongoing struggles about the values that the public, politicians, and educators attach to subjects as they are taught. It is these struggles about values that shape teachers' responses to calls for change and the role of professional learning in changing practice. Teachers are in the unenviable position of often being unfairly portrayed in public as unresponsive to reform while also being cynical of mandated changes that are often driven by political expediency, not evidence. The net result is that the more things change, the more they stay the same.

In this chapter, we will consider four areas that are foundational in helping understand how teachers can answer the calls to better represent scientific activity in their classrooms and departments. The first is to understand the very real cultural issues that act to maintain the status quo in science teaching. The second area is to consider the notion of professional learning in terms of what teachers can do to promote their own sense of professionalism. The third is to consider how the science department can be made to work as a site for professional learning for science teachers. Finally, the fourth area is to consider departmental leadership, which is the responsibility of not just the chair but also individual teachers as they question the status quo of science education, develop models of exemplary practice, and establish the conditions for the ongoing work of improving teaching and learning.

An understanding of these four areas will lead us into the Chapter 3 discussion of the specifics of how teachers can promote their own professional learning within departments before we move on to the experiences of teachers who are working to better represent scientific activity in their departments and classrooms.

Difficult to Change: Understanding Present Practice

The modern science curriculum has been a work in progress since the mid-19th century. The general direction of the curriculum was, however, set out within a few decades of the transformation of natural philosophy into what we now recognize as science. The formation of the British Association for the Advancement of Science (BAAS) in 1831 was a catalyst for institutionalizing many of the attributes of contemporary science. Early protagonists of science, such as William Whewell (1794–1866), actively promoted the superiority of the "pure sciences" over technological applications of science, a status divide that continues to this day. Whewell also coined the term *scientist* in 1834. The decision to subdivide the association's annual meeting into the disciplines still shapes the structure of contemporary science. The newly professionalized science appropriated to itself both disciplinary content and access to the disciplines. The BAAS served as a model for the 1848 formation of the American Association for the Advancement of Science.

The values associated with the professionalization of science have dominated science education over the past 150 years. One of the earliest instances of this domination in Britain came in the shaping of a science curriculum that stressed the values of the BAAS and entrenched the power and prestige of the upper classes. In 1867, the BAAS produced the *Scientific Education in Schools* report. This report was important for two reasons. First, it promoted an elitist professional training of future scientists in the "pure sciences" through mental training (Layton 1981). Second, it established the superiority of disciplinary scientific knowledge: "The education reformers produced a science curriculum that marginalized practical utility and eschewed issues and values related to everyday life, reflecting the BAAS's newly achieved divide between science and technology" (Aikenhead 2006, p. 13).

These purposes of science education also came to dominate in the United States. Although the report of the Committee of Ten (1893) is seen as being particularly influential in shaping the general school curriculum, there is evidence that the impact on science education was more influenced by the disciplinary nature of science and the value attached to the capacity of the disciplines to exercise the mind.

The disciplinary nature of science led to the establishment of a hierarchy of school science subjects: the pure sciences of physics and chemistry, followed by more "practical" sciences such as botany and zoology. This hierarchy was based on the perceived value in developing the mental power of the learner. Biology as a subject did not exist at the time, and there was a functional shift from natural history, with its "study nature not books" pedagogy, to the disciplines of botany and zoology, with their "technical and required laboratory work that was exacting and precise" (Sheppard and Robbins 2007, p. 201). The status of biology as a subject only improved as it began to claim "disciplinary rigor" through the efforts of scientists such as Pasteur and Koch (Goodson 1993).

This notional power of disciplinary rigor continues to be a major impediment to reforming efforts within science education (Carlone 2003). There remains among many teachers and members of the general public a firm view of what a rigorous science education looks like: It is dominated by a mastery of the content and is demonstrated through testing. It is this desire for "good" science teaching that explains the derision that is often displayed toward integrated science subjects and courses seen as "soft science." Further, the continued organization of school science along disciplinary lines is symptomatic of the resilience of the professionalization values, reflecting "the acceptance of … the transmission of certain forms of knowledge. It reflects a view of knowledge that is limited to facts and algorithms" (White 1988, p. 7). Such a view supports, according to Tytler (2007), the contemporary vision of science education:

> The emphasis is on conceptual knowledge, compartmentalised into distinct disciplinary strands, the use of key, abstract concepts to interpret and explain relatively standard problems, the treatment of context as mainly subsidiary to concepts, and the use of practical work to illustrate principles and practices. (p. 3)

Although this may be the current emphasis, the ongoing debate concerning the purposes of science education opens up opportunities for teachers to reconsider the purposes of science education. These opportunities focus on teaching and learning that reflect the epistemic nature of science (ways of coming to know something in science) and the interactions of science, technology, and society emphasized by Latour's (2004) shift from "matters of fact" to "matters of concern." Hodson (2003, 2011) summarized a number of common themes that run through the current iterations of these debates: the meanings of scientific literacy; the relationships between science, technology, society, and the environment; the economic imperatives driving science education; the nature of science; and (pedagogically) how to improve the teaching and learning of science. To meaningfully represent scientific activity in our classrooms, we believe that it is crucial that teachers engage simultaneously with these debates around the purposes of teaching and learning.

Of particular relevance to a push for more authentically representative scientific activity in classrooms as part of a wider reform of science education have been the increasing value of constructivism within science education and greater understanding of the affective dimensions of pedagogy. The past 50 years have also seen a growing public understanding that science is not as monolithic, objective, mechanistic, and decontextualized as it is often portrayed. Science is increasingly understood as subjective, tentative, deeply contextualized, local, and reliant on human inference, creativity, and imagination. This understanding is being driven by the dynamic nature of the enterprise of science and the consequent change in the skills needed by scientists; the changing nature of society's engagement with science; the rise of postmodernist challenges to science; and the explosion in scientific knowledge and the challenges this brings to the traditional transmission model of science teaching (Tytler 2007). In part, these changes are being driven by a questioning of the power of the traditional view of science. For Tytler (2007), this criticism asks: "What can be known and by whom … what constitutes and validates knowledge … [and] raise[s] issues about social context and the status of knowers[?]" (p. 24).

The current reality is that school science has not changed much in the past century and is struggling to engage and retain students in many parts of the Western world. School science, still tied to its historical roots, replicates itself as a system that, although "designed principally to train young people as a preparation for entering the science discipline, is the very instrument that is turning them away from science" (Tytler 2007, p. 18). In part, this is a political issue, as Aikenhead (2006) argues: "The simple ideology of pre-professional training of scientists and engineers seems to have political advantages over more complex ideologies that inspire humanistic approaches to school science" (p. 53). It is this replication of traditional school science that reforms such as the *A Framework for K–12 Science Education* (the *Framework*) and the *Next Generation Science Standards* (*NGSS*) seek to break down. And it is teachers who need to initiate changes in their own understandings and classroom practices.

School science, as it is currently taught, limits teachers' ideas as to "what science is, who does science, what belongs in the science curriculum, and how best to 'deliver' the content" (Carlone 2003, p. 308). Science teachers generally have an "allegiance to teaching facts and to following the role model of college professors" (Welch et al. 1981, p. 40). Constraints such as these develop over time and need to be considered from a variety of perspectives. Such a multifaceted challenge is difficult and starts with science teachers and science teacher educators examining their own beliefs about science. Although "an allegiance to teaching facts" may not accurately reflect your professed views as a science teacher, an unconscious allegiance may still influence teaching and learning in your classroom and in your science department. That influence may come from the beliefs of other teachers in your department, the beliefs of administrators, and the beliefs of the public, which leads to policies that can shape classroom instruction.

This is likely the case because in Western countries the ranks of secondary science teachers are dominated by teachers initially educated in science faculties, a dominance that reflects the academic orientation of science teacher education. This orientation favors a perception of the teacher as a classroom leader and a subject specialist who is well grounded in his or her discipline (Feiman-Nemser 1990). One consequence of this discipline-based education is that science teachers are not *just* teachers—they are teachers of science and hence find it difficult to move toward the teaching and learning promulgated in reform documents such as the *Framework* and the *NGSS*, which emphasize engaging students in developing their facility with scientific practices as they use disciplinary and crosscutting ideas to explain phenomena or solve complex societal issues.

For science education, with its disciplinary roots firmly linked to status and prestige, the pressure on science teachers is to reproduce and secure "the prestige and power of science; it is an education not only *in* science, but also *for* science" (Carlone 2003, p. 310, emphasis in original). Teachers are not, however, entirely powerless against this socializing force. As White (1988) states: "Whatever curriculum writers, politicians, administrators and academics say are the aims of the course, what actually happens is in the hands of teachers" (p. 10). This brings us to the importance of teachers' conceptualization of professional learning and their capacity and ability to shape that learning.

Professional Learning

If we are being honest, the value of much professional learning that occurs in schools can be questioned. The reason for this pessimistic view is that much professional learning fails to address teachers' learning needs, the context of their work, or the ways in which adults learn. Professional learning is not a case of adding new information to teachers' existing knowledge. It is an ongoing cultural task in which teachers need to "change … their perception of the context in which they work" (White 1988, p. 114). And that context, as we have seen, is heavily influenced by the past.

Creating a classroom environment that represents authentic scientific activity is particularly problematic for a number of reasons. To represent scientific activity requires a thorough understanding of the nature of science and a suite of teaching strategies that can be deployed to help students move along the continuum from confirmation to constructing and critiquing explanations (Ford 2008). A further complication is that many people assume that a delivery pedagogy (Stroupe and Windschitl 2015) can be simply adapted to support student learning in representations of scientific activity. Here, there remains an uncertainty among teachers as to what reformers actually mean by authentic representations of scientific activity and how scientific activity might be represented for students in classrooms, and there is a constantly perceived pressure to conform to a traditional view of science education. If they are in doubt as to how to proceed, teachers will understandably revert to teaching the way that they were taught.

The reasoning that supports this (often subconscious) decision includes the perceived difficulty of teaching from a constructivist perspective, the added time and energy that will be needed, and uncertainty regarding how to meet the expectations of the curriculum. Uncertainty regarding the support of colleagues, the perceived physical limitations of the classroom, the costs of apparatus and consumables, a belief that safety will be compromised, the placing of material in the proper sequence, and the demand of preparing students for further study are also cited as concerns (Baker, Lang, and Lawson 2002). One major concern that teachers often express is their uncertainty about the capacity of students to engage with the levels of analysis, argumentation, and evaluation described initially in the *Framework* and the *NGSS*. This uncertainty is understandable but should be viewed in the context of how we currently educate the majority of both secondary school students and university science undergraduates.

To move beyond these legitimate concerns and embrace the representations of scientific activity in classrooms requires teachers to undertake professional learning that addresses these issues. By professional learning, we mean teachers taking responsibility for working together to inquire into their teaching and learning. This emphasis is in line with the National Science Teachers Association (NSTA) *Position Statement on Principles of Professionalism for Science Educators* (see *www.nsta.org/about/positions/professionalism.aspx*). Professional learning requires that teachers ask questions of both their own teaching practices and those of their colleagues, the meanings that they attribute to their work, and the development of identities that support their reformed teaching. The asking of questions into why and how we teach leads to learning and the development of solutions that can be tested and validated. The act of asking questions will begin to change the emphasis of teacher learning more toward that envisioned by the NSTA *Position Statement on Professional Development in Science Education* (see *www.nsta.org/about/positions/profdev.aspx*). This document emphasizes teacher learning through investigation and inquiry, the integration of science and teaching knowledge, the integration of theory and practice, collegial and collaborative learning, long-term coherent planning, a variety of learning activities, and an appropriate mix of internal and external expertise. These emphases have been considered by different teachers at different stages in their careers in their vignettes found beginning in Chapter 4.

The long-term aim of professional learning should be to align teachers' understanding of science education and classroom practices with the vision of the *Framework* and the *NGSS*. This alignment will require teachers to develop a rich understanding of the nature of science and the disciplinary core ideas, crosscutting concepts, and science and engineering practices they are expected to teach. To translate this knowledge into the classroom will require teachers to be able to draw on a range of appropriate instructional strategies that support teaching, learning, and assessment in this newly envisioned environment. It is this sense of developing alignment that will become clearer through the teachers' vignettes that follow in Chapters 4 through 7. A commitment to the long term for professional learning is important, as are leadership; a clear sense of purpose; and a willingness to challenge both individual and shared tightly held teaching beliefs, practices, and knowledge. To expect individual teachers to make these changes without support is unrealistic and goes against everything that we know about how teachers learn. Recognizing this brings us to the department as a logical site for teacher professional learning.

The Importance of the Science Department

School subject departments are a ubiquitous feature of secondary schools throughout the world. Although they are usually perceived as convenient administrative units, there is growing evidence of their potential as sites of teacher professional learning. Central to realizing this potential is the role of teacher leaders in modeling, establishing, and maintaining the intellectual and social conditions under which teachers can engage in meaningful, sustained, professional learning (Brundrett and Terrell 2004). Equally important is an understanding that departments operate simultaneously as both organizations and communities (Melville and Wallace 2007). As organizations, departments possess political power, concerning themselves with the "control of territory, the distribution of resources, the acquisition of status, and participation in the decision-making process" (Blenkin, Edwards, and Kelly 1997, p. 222). This concern must, however, be tempered by the realization that power is contextualized within the community and must therefore be responsive to the needs and desires of that community. As communities, departments are a context for the development of teacher identities, meanings, and practices. This context must therefore provide opportunities for teachers to critically reflect on the work of both themselves and their colleagues.

Science departments hold an inordinate amount of influence over the teaching and learning of the teachers who inhabit them. Tytler (2007) describes the contemporary situation for the majority of science teachers succinctly:

> Part of the reason for the persistence of status quo science relates to the strong discursive traditions subscribed to by teachers of science resulting from their enculturation during their own schooling and undergraduate studies. ... This culture is strongly represented in school science discursive practices, supported by resources such as textbooks,

*laboratories and their associated equipment, timetabling arrangements
and by assessment and reporting traditions. Another aspect is the force
of long habit of teachers who have developed effective ways of delivering
canonical content, who may lack the knowledge, skills and perspectives
required for the effective teaching of a different version of school science.
(p. 18)*

Teachers need to understand that their departments have the potential to either
encourage the replication of a traditional science education or become centers for
professional learning that support and encourage the version of school science envisioned in the *Framework* and the *NGSS*. To develop departments that are supportive
of their professional learning, teachers need to reconsider their relationship with the
department. There are two dominant ways in which teachers define their relationship with the department, and these are directly related to teachers' views of science.

In their work on teacher learning, Wildy and Wallace (2004) state that "teachers within the same discipline do not always share the same views about what
constitutes good teaching" or the same views as to the "nature of science itself"
(p. 100). This is not meant to imply that teachers' views are static or that teachers
are incapable of change. Teachers who perceive science as "a set of universal truths
that describe the operation of the natural world" also tend to view the purpose of
school science as the traditional "delivery of that knowledge" (p. 109). The alternative description of science is "as a process of personal sense making that helps
people survive in their environment" (p. 109); this view appears to be more commonly held by teachers more disposed toward constructivist pedagogies.

Flowing from these two perceptions of the discipline of science have come two
conceptions of work in the science department. Under the first perception of science, the science department "is a tightly organised and orderly place to work.
There is one best way of teaching and a single best way of assessing students'
learning" (Wildy and Wallace 2004, p. 109). Alternatively, the second description
of science recounts the science department as one in which "the goals of inquiry,
individuality and freedom sought for students in the classroom are also sought
for teachers in the department" (p. 109). In dealing with these contradictions—
and their implication for the development of a departmental culture that supports
professional learning—teachers will need to confront the values that they hold. As
Brundrett and Terrell (2004) state,

*This process is a moral and a political one because it involves the
creating, organising, managing, monitoring and resolving of value
conflicts, where values are defined as concepts of the desirable ... and
power is used to implement some values rather than others. (p. 17)*

One of the issues that has been captured in the vignettes is how teachers respond to the contradictions involved in these conceptions and how those in leadership positions have actively worked through those contradictions.

Leadership

Leadership within departments is important, but it is increasingly being seen as based less on a hierarchy of power and more as based on a hierarchy in which authority is derived from the development of a shared sense of ideals for the teaching and learning of the subject. Formally designated authority positions, such as the departmental chair, necessarily contain a number of administrative management functions that are vital to the operation of the department, but leadership is different. If a department is to start moving toward the concepts of science teaching and learning envisioned in the *Framework* and the *NGSS*, then leadership will be required. Regardless of how tentative the first steps in the journey are, the time and effort that will be needed to lead a department should not be seen as more work; it is a different form of work.

Implementation of the *Framework* and the *NGSS* will require teachers to develop an understanding of how scientific activity can be represented in their classrooms. The development of this understanding is important for two reasons. The first is that teachers value credibility; far too often, reforms have been promoted that have not taken how teachers learn into account. Teachers need time to experiment and refine new practices. Through this iterative process, teachers can become "a credible source for advice on instructional matters wherein one's expertise is acknowledged ... and thus, the person finds themselves in a leadership role" (Judson and Lawson 2007, p. 501).

Leadership is about individuals who model exemplary teaching and learning practices with the intention of promoting similar practices among their colleagues, thus improving the practice of all. Riley (2000) has argued that "successful school leaders model professional values and aspirations, supporting teachers in meeting professional challenges and in managing the change process" (p. 48). Modeling practice is fundamentally different from the simple sharing of practice, as it is reliant on the development of high-quality relationships between members of the department. As Fielding et al. (2005) note,

> The development and/or continuity of certain kinds of trusting relationships are fundamental to the transfer of good practice. They are not a welcome extra or a pleasant accompaniment, but the necessary foundation of the complex, demanding and potentially rewarding process of professional learning. (p. 74)

Second, leadership cannot be imposed; it emerges as teachers begin to develop their own expertise. Departmental leadership requires the courage to question the status quo of science education in both the classroom and the wider department. To question is important, for it is through questioning that alternatives can be explored. As Cochran-Smith and Lytle (1999) explain, questioning makes "tacit knowledge more visible, calls into question assumptions about common practices ... and [makes] possible the consideration of alternatives" (p. 294). For a department to make substantive progress in implementing the *Framework* and the *NGSS*, however, requires the chair (or whoever has formal authority in the department) to take the initiative in developing the conditions in which this questioning and experimentation can flourish—which brings us to the role of the science chair.

Developing and modeling exemplary teaching, questioning both individual and departmental practice, and establishing the conditions for others to question their practice are all foundational to the wider implementation of improvements to teaching and learning. Cochran-Smith and Lytle (1999) argue that "teachers learn collaboratively ... [when] participants struggle along with others to construct meaningful local knowledge and where inquiry is regarded as part of larger efforts to transform teaching, learning and schooling" (p. 278). This has profound implications for the position and work of the chair. The former British Teacher Training Agency (1998) summarized that work as follows:

> *A subject leader has responsibility for securing high standards in teaching and learning in their subject as well as playing a major role in the development of school policy and practice. Throughout their work, a subject leader ensures that practices improve the quality of education provided, meet the needs and aspirations of all pupils, and raise standards of achievement in the school. (p. 4)*

The literature on departmental leadership (see Rennie 2010) indicates that to begin to fulfill these responsibilities, chairs need to be actively working with their departments in a number of areas. The overarching goal of departmental leadership, however, is the cultivation of a critical moral view of education (Brundrett and Terrell 2004).

In accepting this position, we are stating that fundamental change in science teaching will be achieved through departments exhibiting leadership that is built around the values of the practices that can support more authentic representations of scientific activity in classrooms as envisioned in the *Framework* and the *NGSS*. Further, we believe that the potential impact of the chair is diminished when he or she only functions in an administrative role and forgoes the role of professional learner and leader in focusing his or her own attention—and that of his or her colleagues—on professional growth with respect to teaching and learning.

Conclusion

The purpose of this chapter has been to outline four foundational issues that influence teaching and learning. The first two issues are the deep-seated cultural pressures to conform to a traditional view of the science curriculum and the notion of teacher professional learning and how teachers need to take the initiative and assume responsibility for addressing their own questions of practice, meaning, and identity. The third is to view the science department—a ubiquitous feature of most secondary schools—as a potentially powerful site for professional learning. Finally, we considered the role of leadership, a role that requires questioning, the development and modeling of exemplary practice, and establishing the conditions for the ongoing work of improving teaching and learning.

In Chapter 3, these ideas will be extended using the framework developed by Timperley et al. (2007), which highlights four fundamental components of a framework for analyzing the efficacy of professional learning experiences: (1) the professional learning context, (2) the content of the professional learning opportunities, (3) the activities that are constructed to promote learning, and (4) the learning processes that teachers engage in. These components will then form the basis for the teacher vignettes that start in Chapter 4. But first, the following are the most salient takeaways from this chapter. We also provide questions that can be used to promote collaborative reflection and discussion within the department.

Summary

- There remains among many teachers and members of the general public a firm view of what a rigorous science education looks like: It is dominated by a mastery of the content that is demonstrated through testing.

- Science teachers generally have an "allegiance to teaching facts and to following the role model of college professors" (Welch et al. 1981, p. 40). Although this may not accurately reflect your views as a science teacher, it may still influence teaching and learning in your classroom and science department. That influence may come from the beliefs of other teachers in your department, the beliefs of administrators, and the beliefs of the public and leads to policies that can shape classroom instruction.

- Moving beyond legitimate concerns (e.g., time, support, physical limitations of classrooms, concerns for safety) and embracing the representations of scientific activity in classrooms requires teachers to undertake professional learning that addresses these concerns.

- Professional learning involves teachers taking responsibility for working together to inquire into their teaching and learning and requires that teachers ask questions of both their own teaching practices and those of their colleagues, the meanings that they attribute to their work, and the development of identities that support their reformed teaching practices.

- There is growing evidence of the potential of science departments to serve as sites of teacher professional learning. Central to realizing this potential is the role of teacher leaders in modeling, establishing, and maintaining the intellectual and social conditions under which teachers can engage in meaningful and sustained professional learning.

- Science departments hold an inordinate amount of influence over the teaching and learning of the teachers who inhabit them.

- Teachers need to understand that their departments have the potential to become centers for professional learning that supports and encourages the version of school science envisioned in the *Framework* and the *NGSS*; otherwise, they will remain static in replicating a traditional science education that is increasingly indefensible.

- The leadership of the department is an important role, but it is increasingly being seen as a role based less on a hierarchy of power and more as a role in which authority is derived from the development of a shared sense of ideals for teaching and learning of the subject.

- Leadership is about individuals who model exemplary teaching and learning practices with the intention of promoting similar practices among their colleagues, thus improving the practice of all.

Questions to Consider

1. Where are the remnants of the firm view of science education (i.e., dominated by mastery of content and demonstrated through testing) most pervasive in your department, school, district, or community? For those that are recognized as exerting pressure on teaching and learning in the classroom, what role can the department play in helping refocus this view to better align with the *Framework* and the *NGSS*?

2. What are the most pressing legitimate concerns that need to be addressed for teachers in the department to embrace professional learning around the representation of scientific activity in classrooms? What are some early ideas for negotiating the concerns identified?

3. To what extent can teacher leaders be found in your department or school who model, establish, and maintain the intellectual and social conditions under which teachers can engage in meaningful, sustained, professional learning? What are ways to support others within the department in the work of becoming teacher leaders?

4. What are ways in which your department serves as a center for professional learning to support and encourage the version of school science envisioned in the *Framework* and the *NGSS*? What are additional ways the department can offer support in realizing these visions?

5. How might the development of a shared sense of ideals for teaching and learning of science be further cultivated within your department?

Building the Conditions for Learning

In this chapter, we would like to provide a framework for considering the professional learning conditions within departments that are most supportive of teachers who are working to engage their students in classroom versions of scientific activity. Wilson and Berne (1999) write at length as to how teachers' professional learning needs to incorporate opportunities for teachers to talk about their subject, their students and how they learn, and their own teaching. Unfortunately, many past and present professional learning opportunities have relied on lecturing to teachers rather than developing teachers' capacity to engage in critical conversations.

Professional learning opportunities need to give teachers the capacity to question the practices for themselves and their department, and from there develop new insights and practices that can be tested and validated in the context of classrooms with students. Such conversations will, over time, also develop a shared knowledge about engaging students in representations of scientific activity that will influence how individual teachers view their students and their professional learning. Much of this knowledge is tacit and, as such, is difficult to share explicitly. By developing opportunities to understand students and their learning, teachers can begin to integrate their evolving beliefs about scientific activity into their everyday teaching practices as they work to engage students in practices comparable with those scientists use for working at knowing (i.e., science and engineering practices) to use ideas (e.g., everyday ways of using language, partial understandings, disciplinary core ideas, crosscutting concepts) to make sense of the world around them.

One of the reasons that science as inquiry made little impact in classrooms was a general "overemphasis by teachers, curricula, and textbooks on what we know at the expense of how we know" (Osborne 2010, p. 464). As a consequence, school science has come to be characterized as discipline-based conceptual knowledge that has little connection to students' lives and experiences. This is an ongoing issue and one that *A Framework for K–12 Science Education* (the *Framework*) and the *Next Generation Science Standards* (*NGSS*) attempt to address by recognizing that the goal of instruction needs to shift from learning about disciplinary content or facts to instead using and refining ideas to explain phenomena (Reiser 2013). One powerful way to overcome this overemphasis on facts in science teaching is to develop a shared knowledge base that addresses issues of student learning within a coherent professional learning structure. Encouraging teachers to talk about teaching in the context of their everyday work opens up opportunities for teachers to begin to exercise control over their work: one of the signs of a profession. With commitment and leadership, teachers can make the change from being the targets of professional development to shaping and leading their own professional learning, especially as they consider the following research-based recommendations for professional learning that can support the visions of science teaching and learning outlined in the *NGSS:* "Structure teacher sense-making around rich images of classroom … [and] structure teachers' work to be collaborative efforts to apply *NGSS* to their own classrooms" (Reiser 2013, pp. 15–16).

As we discussed in Chapter 2, the science department is a potentially powerful site for initiating and sustaining these changes in the emphases of professional learning conversations. We say *potentially*, as there appears to be a number of issues that arise when considering professional learning and departments. There are powerful structural and cultural forces to acknowledge and move beyond, and it is also necessary to recognize that teachers within the department will need to work together to align their views on science education, classroom needs, and practices with the vision of the *Framework* and the *NGSS*. It is unrealistic to expect an individual teacher to build the knowledge that we have talked about here and then enact it in his or her classroom without support from his or her colleagues in considering the many policies, structures, and cultural commitments within schools that might be prohibitive of such work. Working together provides the opportunities teachers will need to not only address systemic constraints that might inhibit change but also develop a deep understanding of the scientific ideas and practices they are expected to teach and also develop and validate during their course work. This includes a wide range of instructional strategies that support the teaching, learning, and assessment of students' engagement in their guided or self-directed attempts to emulate representations of scientific activity.

It is all well and good to speak in generalities of teachers working together within their department to frame student learning as engagement in classroom versions of scientific activity. The question is "How can teachers begin to build these opportunities within their department, and what conditions will support this work?" It is time to move from the general to the specific if departments are to exploit their potential as places in which teacher professional learning can prosper.

A Framework for Professional Learning

To be specific about the conditions that support teacher professional learning, we will be using the synthesis study conducted by Timperley et al. (2007). This work synthesized a number of studies into the opportunities and processes that influence teacher professional learning and, consequently, student learning. This synthesis highlighted the four basic components of effective professional learning opportunities:

1. Professional learning context

2. Content of the professional learning opportunities

3. Activities that promote professional learning

4. Learning processes that teachers engage in

For each of these components of professional learning, the synthesis identified specific constituent areas that can be considered to have an impact "in terms of changing the teaching of science in ways that led to positive outcomes for students" (Timperley et al. 2007, p. 103). In the next four sections, we will discuss each component and the links between their constituent areas. The components, constituent areas, and associated descriptors can be found in the appendix (p. 137). At this point, we would also suggest you take a look at the NSTA *Position Statement on Professional Development in Science Education* (see *www.nsta.org/about/positions/profdev.aspx*).

One danger of providing lists of conditions that support a framework for professional learning is that they can become unwieldy and simply overwhelm the reader. They can then be effectively ignored. No one expects that any department would, or could, commit to all of the specific areas at once. It is simply not possible, nor reasonable, to expect teachers to change their practices overnight. The vignettes in Chapters 4 through 7 will demonstrate that teachers can, and do, make great progress by incrementally transforming their teaching and learning. By gradually developing their expertise in representing scientific activity, they are better prepared to take on the ambitious challenge of transforming science learning in schools. Our advice would be to look over the professional learning framework components and their constituent areas and carefully consider where you and your department are already making progress (or could realistically make progress in the short term) and then, in light of the vignettes, consider what professional learning your department could most confidently address. Each department will start in a different place and move at different speeds along different paths but toward the same goal. There will be backtracking, cul-de-sacs, and dead ends, but these are all important, as they shape and fortify those strategies that take hold and are able to meet departmental needs.

The Professional Learning Context

In this section, we wish to consider the following constituent areas of the professional learning context of the department:

1. Coherence with policy

2. Prevailing discourses

3. Professional learning goals

4. Time and frequency

5. External expertise

6. Infrastructural supports

7. School leadership

8. Voluntary or compulsory involvement

In considering these areas, we are interested in how they interact with one another and also offer some guidance in how they can be understood.

Understanding the professional learning context of your department is critical in deciding how to implement the potentially dramatic shifts in instruction called for by the *Framework* and the *NGSS*. Each of the Chapter 4 vignettes demonstrates that all teachers, regardless of their classroom experience or position within the department, understand at least some of the conditions under which they work. Importantly, the more experienced teachers and chairs look beyond the surface appearances of the context and understand the history, politics, and personalities involved in shaping the contemporary context. For further reading on the topic, please refer to the National Research Council's 2015 book, *Science Teachers' Learning: Enhancing Opportunities, Creating Supportive Contexts,* available as a free download from *www.nap.edu/catalog/21836/ science-teachers-learning-enhancing-opportunities-creating-supportive-contexts.*

It is important to understand that any move to change teachers' practices needs to be made in *coherence with policy* documents. By coherence, we mean that teachers need to work at developing clear connections among their work, the work of their students, and the vision of science education promoted by the *Framework* and the *NGSS.* Reform documents by themselves will not produce change—they provide a research-based framework within which teachers can work to reform their instructional practices. As Timperley et al. (2007) state, "It is significant that all cases of professional development that led to positive outcomes for students were part of wider and coherent movements in science teaching and learning that were underpinned by strong research bases" (p. 105).

Seen this way, documents such as the *Framework* and the *NGSS* raise two questions for teachers looking to engage students in representations of scientific activity. The first is "How well do I understand the *Framework* and the *NGSS* in both theory and practice?" The second question is closely related to this: "How well do my colleagues understand documents such as the *Framework* and the *NGSS* in both theory and practice?"

Answering these questions is, in many ways, foundational to understanding the next two areas. These areas are understanding the *prevailing discourses* of science education that are held by science teachers, the practices that exemplify these discourses, and the specific *professional learning goals* that underpin any move to incorporate three-dimensional learning—the prevailing discourse of the *Framework* and the *NGSS*—into teaching and learning. Three-dimensional learning, as articulated in Chapter 1, is understood in the *Framework* and the *NGSS* as engaging students in science and engineering practices to use disciplinary core ideas and crosscutting concepts to explain phenomena or solve problems. As we have already discussed, teachers experience significant difficulty in reforming their practices unless they can understand why the change is being made, understand how the change fits with a new (or, more accurately, developing) understanding of science education, accept that the change is credible in terms of the classroom, and validate the change in terms of teaching and learning.

The fourth area is the need for professional learning to be given *frequent attention and time* to make a sustained difference to teaching and learning. Each of the Chapter 4 vignettes makes this point abundantly clear. As teachers, we need to stop rushing between the latest fads (be they mandate, content, equipment, or teaching strategy) and focus on what is important in our work. Attention to professional learning is particularly important during the early stages of any change, which can last three or four years. Short-term changes are likely to have a limited impact, even as they continue to be the standard professional development offering. For a damning indictment of contemporary professional learning, see Darling-Hammond and Sykes (1999), who fault current practices for

> focusing on district-mandated, generic instructional skills of teachers
> "trained" as individuals by an outside "expert" away from their job
> site. Because this training is fragmented, piecemeal, and often based on
> instructional fads, it is viewed as a frill, easily dispensed with in tough
> financial times. Perhaps most damaging, these workshops, although they

*often respond to expressed teacher needs, are seldom explicitly linked to
what schools expect students know and be able to do. (p. 134)*

Sadly, this was written 18 years ago. On a more positive note, *external expertise*
can benefit departments that are looking to reform (or refine) their teaching and
learning. Such expertise can come in many forms: subject associations such as the
National Science Teachers Assocaition (NSTA), board and curriculum offices, universities and colleges, volunteer organizations, or private enterprise. Again, each of
the Chapter 4 vignettes highlights the value of being actively involved in working
with outside expertise to build the professional learning capacity of a department.
Do not discount the teacher who is undertaking professional learning in other contexts. Instead, ask how he or she can contribute to the department and "what and
how can we learn from them?"

An often overlooked area that can have an impact are the *infrastructural supports*
that school administrators can offer in terms of political support, funding, support
for board-level initiatives, and release time. One strategy for securing this support
is to keep administrators and the *school leadership* in the loop as to what is happening within the department and to invite them to professional learning activities as
appropriate. All of our contributing teachers have actively sought out the support
of school administrators and have worked to develop a high level of relational trust
with them. Finally, the vexed question of *teacher involvement* in professional learning is more nuanced than we might expect. There is clearly a personal element here
for those who would seek to build professional learning within a department, and
it revolves around how well teachers know and trust each other. If teachers volunteer to work toward reforming their practices, there is still no guarantee that they
will make significant change.

Volunteering is certainly preferable to being "voluntold," but what is "important is that teachers 'buy in' at some point. Buy-in is related more to the content and
form of the professional learning than to whether teachers do or do not volunteer"
(Timperley et al. 2007, p. 105). That leads us to the second basic component of effective professional learning opportunities: content.

The Content of Professional Learning

Science teachers tend to have an academic orientation to teaching, a factor closely
related to the historical nature of the subject in schools. For example, Australian science department chairs have been shown to overwhelming prefer newly appointed
teachers to have an undergraduate degree in science, followed by a teaching certi-
fication, as this brings with it the promise of greater depth of scientific knowledge
(Harris, Jensz, and Baldwin 2005). Throughout most states in the United States, an
undergraduate degree in science is not required, but stringent content preparation

is mandated. The content preparation for most science teachers in the United States is the responsibility of university science faculties. The situation is similar in Canada.

These preferences and requirements reinforce the abstract, discipline-bound understanding of science that dominates school and university science education. Teachers who have been largely socialized in their own science course work by the almost exclusive focus on content through delivery pedagogy in science faculties have learned and refined traditional strategies for perpetuating this form of scientific knowledge. Consequently, through no fault of their own, teachers may lack the necessary understanding, pedagogical knowledge, and skills needed to teach in ways that more authentically represent scientific activity in meaningful, coherent ways. As Reiser (2013) explains, such a change

> requires teachers and textbooks not to simply present facts and definitions as ends in themselves, but rather to help students continually work toward explanatory models, developing these ideas from evidence … from _learning about_ scientific ideas such as cells to _figuring out_ scientific ideas that explain how and why phenomena occur. … Teachers need to see targets of learning such as cells as explanations for phenomena, and need to enact lessons in which they help students develop, test, and refine these explanatory ideas. This focus on developing explanations poses challenges for teachers in how to motivate lessons through phenomena that need to be explained, how to help learners develop these explanations, and tie them to the phenomena and questions that motivated them. (p. 4, emphasis in the original)

When we discuss the content of professional learning, we need to be clear that we are not talking about simply adding more content knowledge. By content, we are talking about opportunities for teacher professional learning that engages teachers as learners in scientific activity and then supports them when they engage with their students in developing explanatory accounts of real-world phenomena.

Therefore, in this section we wish to consider the following areas that, taken together, constitute the content of professional learning opportunities within the department:

1. Pedagogical content knowledge

2. Integration of theory and practice

3. Knowledge of assessment

4. Content to support a particular program

If teachers are to work from the *Framework* and the *NGSS,* then "from a learning perspective, the way to develop robust flexible knowledge is to build that knowledge as part of applying it to solve problems and questions about the world" (Reiser 2013, p. 7). From the framework developed by Timperley et al. (2007), we are talking about building teachers' *pedagogical content knowledge,* the importance of which is illustrated when "a teacher realized that, while she had been a successful science student herself, the kind of content knowledge she had was not necessarily the right kind for an inquiry-based approach, which valued understanding over memorization" (p. 111).

An emphasis on pedagogical content knowledge will also concern itself with more than theory. It is not enough to give teachers theory and expect that it will be applied in the classroom; there must be an *integration of theory and practice.* As Reiser (2013) explains:

> *One challenging aspect of supporting practices is understanding how the practices work together. Although* NGSS *is developed using eight practices, these are identified to specify the different types of activity that need to work together to build, test, and refine knowledge. In fact, these eight practices constitute a single system of sense-making. The practices need to work together to be coherent. (p. 7)*

If a teacher or department is looking to incorporate student experiences that approximate scientific activity, then that would indicate dissatisfaction with current practices. The next step in changing practice, according to Posner et al. (1982), is to make sense of the change—a process in which experience and new knowledge are applied to the change and possibilities are explored. This does not mean that we can simply replace current practice with reformed practice—change in science education is more give and take, as it requires a "process of weighing alternates and evaluating the balance of probabilities between two competing beliefs" (Henderson et al. 2015, p. 1676). Following this, the change must be seen as plausible and capable of solving teachers' instructional issues. This is one of the reasons why the teachers' vignettes in Chapter 5 will deal with incremental change as the teachers work to solve issues of how to integrate the pedagogy of scientific activity with authentic classroom practices to support sense making by explaining phenomena or solving problems. The final stage of the process is to reimagine how teachers perceive change and open up new possibilities for inquiry.

This brings us to the level of understanding and knowledge that teachers have about the aims and uses of *assessment.* A major concern for teachers looking to implement the *Framework* and the *NGSS* is how to conduct assessments that reflect scientific activity and are seen (by themselves, administrators, and the wider public) as rigorous (see the NSTA *Position Statement on Assessment* at *www.nsta.org/*

about/positions/assessment.aspx). The focus on students' conceptual understanding means that teachers need to reconsider both the content and use of their assessment tools and clearly link those tools to the teaching of scientific sense making. This is an ongoing issue for teachers and also a source of friction when the assessment strategies that teachers consider most appropriate for understanding student learning in the context of scientific activity run counter to mandated testing regimes.

The final area of professional learning content is the need to *support a particular program*. The *Framework* and the *NGSS* do not mandate a specific program in the traditional sense; rather, they seek to align the teaching and learning of science in schools with student experiences that more accurately represent science disciplines, both in how science practices are employed and in how these are used to construct and critique explanations. For this reason, they will constantly be a work in progress, being shaped as teachers use them and develop strategies that meet the particular needs of their students. There really is no definitive answer as to how student versions of scientific activity will evolve and operate in individual schools. The Chapter 5 vignettes highlight this diversity of implementation that is necessarily context dependent to focus on the needs and resources of students (e.g., cultural and linguistic resources) and schools (i.e., place-based resources).

Activities That Promote Professional Learning

Professional learning can involve teachers in a range of activities, from the much-maligned expert-led workshop to long-term strategies such as mentoring. Reiser (2013) clearly identifies that professional learning opportunities need to include activities that are grounded in the subject, actively engage teachers in problem solving and sense making, and connect to teachers' practices. Similarly, Timperley et al. (2007, p. 115) noted eight areas that need to be considered if activities are to promote teacher professional learning:

1. Sequencing of activities

2. Activities to translate theory into practice

3. Demonstrations of classroom practice

4. Receiving instructional materials

5. Being observed and receiving feedback

6. Engaging with professional readings

7. Comparing own theories with new theories

8. Participating in professional communities

In considering the range of professional learning activities that are available, we would make two observations. The first is that no single activity, or sequence of activities, is guaranteed to promote professional learning within a department. This means that those individuals looking to promote teaching and learning will need to investigate the professional learning needs of their colleagues and tailor their activities to those needs. The vignettes in Chapter 6 will demonstrate this need to be open to the various needs of the teachers who constitute the department. The second observation is that the types of activities that are undertaken should not be static; the learning needs of teachers evolve, and so should the professional learning activities that they engage in. Again, the Chapter 6 vignettes will highlight these developments. With these thoughts in mind, we are now in a position to consider what the research tells us about the professional learning activities that are most effective for improving teaching and learning.

To promote professional learning, there is a need to *sequence activities* to provide both knowledge and understanding to teachers and then the opportunity, time, and support to *translate* the new knowledge and understanding into classroom practice. As Reiser (2013) states, professional learning activities need to

> *involve* active sense-making and problem solving *(Garet, Porter, Desimone, Birman and Yoon 2001). Teachers, like all learners, must go beyond being presented with ideas and strategies; they need the opportunity to analyze cases and apply the strategies themselves. (p. 13, emphasis in the original)*

Huberman (1992) describes this process as "tinkering" (p. 137), and it is through tinkering that teachers make sense of complex ideas: "An individualised embryo of knowledge creation [which if] more systematic, more collective and explicitly managed … is transformed into knowledge creation" (Hargreaves 2000, p. 231).

Translating reforms from pages in a document into the classroom necessitates time and a range of activities to be available for teachers. Teachers learn in different ways—a fact that is not always acknowledged in traditional professional development programs.

Also, remember that teachers, like all learners, require multiple opportunities to apply their new learning across different contexts; this is best accomplished with support during these enactments. The activities that promote learning need to be active and linked to teachers' practices. As such, these activities can include but are certainly not limited to *demonstrations of classroom practice* that teachers can observe and critique; the *provision of instructional materials,* with the understanding that provision by itself is insufficient for learning to occur; the *opportunity to be observed* in a nonevaluative way and discuss the observation; *engaging with professional readings* in science education; and conversations around *existing theories of teaching and learning* and how these relate to, or are challenged by, engaging students in representations of scientific activity. The guiding principle of these activities should be to begin to see teachers

> less as consumers and more as providers of knowledge concerning teaching. Teachers are portrayed less as followers and more as leaders. They are seen less as persons housed in a classroom and more as a member of a professional community. The teacher is not seen as "the target" for change, but as a source and facilitator of change. (Yager 2005, p. 18)

This brings us to the final area that has been identified as promoting professional learning: active *participation* in professional communities. First and foremost, the science department should serve as a professional community as we discussed in Chapter 2: a place in which teachers can share and challenge their beliefs, experiences, and practices and where they can ultimately support and learn from their colleagues. Teachers should also consider other forms of professional community. Professional associations such as NSTA have a number of regional bodies; there are numerous state-based organizations; the Canadian provinces have science teachers' associations; and the Association for Science Education in the United Kingdom has a distinguished history in promoting science teaching and learning. There are also a number of discipline-specific associations that teachers might wish to join. As the Chapter 6 vignettes will demonstrate, the point is to actively participate in the profession. One key strategy by which professional associations promote teaching and learning is in giving their members access to new knowledge and to the experiences of other teachers who are focused on implementing the *NGSS*. Learning processes are the final condition for professional learning outlined by Timperley et al. (2007).

Learning Processes

One key thread running through the literature on professional learning is that changes to teaching and learning do not occur by simply giving teachers information. Timperley et al. (2007) noted three areas that need to be considered if activities are to promote teacher professional learning:

1. New information

2. Creating dissonance with current position (values and beliefs)

3. Consolidating prior knowledge

Change is a process that involves recognizing the need to change, accessing information about alternatives to the status quo, understanding what the change may mean to practice, working incrementally to incorporate the change into practice, and then evaluating the efficacy of the change. Such a process requires time and, to improve the chances of success, the support of our teaching colleagues. Developing strategies to work through the processes of change is clearly important and, to this end, knowing *how* to use information is crucial.

When considering *new information,* we need to ensure that our understanding of the information is more than superficial. Education fads come and go, to the extent that we can become cynical of yet another reform. Such cynicism can be dangerous, as it can stop us from working to develop a deeper understanding of the challenges that we face in our instruction. Acting on new information can guide how to build, both intellectually and practically, ways of representing and supporting students' work in scientific activity inside classrooms. Data can come from a variety of sources: school-level enrollment figures, student course selections, and the destinations of students as they leave school. How teachers access those information sources, and what they do with them, is one of the consistent themes in the Chapter 6 vignettes.

Developing a deeper understanding of new information has value when it causes *dissonance* between current values and practices and the proposed change. As we have seen, implementing the *Framework* and the *NGSS* will be challenging for a number of reasons. Too often in the past, reforms have been proposed that have been rejected on the grounds that they were not seen as credible, had been developed in an ivory tower and were therefore impractical, or had been tried (often once) before and didn't work. One purpose of the Chapter 7 vignettes is to personalize the challenges of working to integrate reformed visions of science teaching and learning into the day-to-day work of science teachers—in other words, to *consolidate prior knowledge* in light of the reform. The struggles of the teachers are real, as are the benefits to teaching and learning that they have realized so far, and they all started by being challenged in what they were doing. Information by itself is useless; it must be evaluated in light of current instructional practice and then be given the opportunity to act as a foundation for incremental changes that improve the teaching and learning of science.

Conclusion

This summary of the components (context, content, activities, and learning processes) that support teacher professional learning provides a framework for considering the experiences of the teachers whose stories follow. A specific framework is essential, we believe, as it allows us to focus on those experiences that may be common to teachers regardless of where they are in their careers, as well as those nuanced experiences that are often critical in helping teachers challenge their teaching and learning and so begin the task of improving their practices.

Summary

- Teacher professional learning needs to incorporate opportunities for teachers to talk about their subject, their students and how they learn, and their own teaching. Encouraging teachers to talk about teaching in the context of their everyday work opens up opportunities for teachers to begin to exercise control over their work: one of the signs of a profession.

- With commitment and leadership, teachers can make the change from being the targets of professional development to shaping and leading their own professional learning, especially as they consider the following research-based recommendations for professional learning that can support the visions of science teaching and learning as outlined in the *NGSS:* "Structure teacher sense-making around rich images of classroom … [and] structure teachers' work to be collaborative efforts to apply *NGSS* to their own classrooms" (Reiser 2013, pp. 15–16).

- It is unrealistic to expect an individual teacher to build knowledge around the *NGSS* and then enact it in his or her classroom without support from his or her colleagues in considering the many policies, structures, and cultural commitments within schools that might be prohibitive of such work.

- It is important to understand that any move to change teachers' practices needs to be made in *coherence with policy* documents. By coherence, we mean that teachers need to work at developing clear connections between their work, the work of their students, and the vision of science education promoted by the *Framework* and the *NGSS.*

- The *Framework* and the *NGSS* do not mandate a specific program in the traditional sense; rather, they seek to align the teaching and learning of science in schools with student experiences that more accurately represent science disciplines, both in how science practices are employed and in how these are used to construct and critique explanations.

- Professional learning opportunities need to include activities that are grounded in the subject, actively engage teachers in problem solving and sense making, and are connected to teachers' practices. Like all learners, teachers require multiple opportunities to apply their new learning across different contexts, and this is best accomplished with support during these enactments.

- Information by itself is useless; it must be evaluated in light of current instructional practice and then be given the opportunity to act as a foundation for incremental changes that improve the teaching and learning of science.

Questions to Consider

1. What are ways your department can intentionally foster opportunities for teachers to talk about their subject, their students and how they learn, and their own teaching in the context of their everyday work?

2. How can teachers in the department be supported to shape and lead professional learning focused on "teacher sense-making around rich images of classroom … [and] collaborative efforts to apply *NGSS* to their own classrooms" (Reiser 2013, pp. 15–16)?

3. What are ways in which teachers can collaborate to support one another in clearly connecting their work, the work of their students, and the vision of the *Framework* and the *NGSS* for science teaching and learning?

4. What strategies can your department identify for more accurately representing science disciplines, both in how science practices are employed and in how these are used to construct and critique explanations?

5. Because teachers as learners require multiple opportunities to apply their new learning across different contexts, which is best accomplished with support during these enactments, what are some arrangements that can be made that will offer teachers support during their enactments of the *NGSS?*

6. Can you identify an incremental approach that is guiding your school's or department's improvement in teaching and learning science? If so, is this approach made explicit for all to see and understand? If not, how might you facilitate the articulation and pursuit of an incremental approach for your school or department?

The Professional Learning Context

The learning context, for Timperley et al. (2007), is where professional learning opportunities occur that "work in terms of changing the teaching of science in ways that [lead] to positive outcomes for students" (p. 103). To build the department as a professional learning context is to move toward a place where teachers learn to work together to improve the teaching and learning that occurs in their school. In the words of Jason, such a department is one in which

> teachers plan together and teach together. Instead of one teacher trying to learn new strategies in their class alone, all teachers in the department help facilitate their learning. Then the risk (and potential reward) is shared by all. Teachers learn that it is all right to be critical of the strategy or flaws in their planning. And teachers were thinking of how to do it better the next time, even if things didn't go as well as they wanted it to. Discussions were rich, frank, and productive.

Such a context does not occur by chance, but how is it perceived and even supported by teachers at different stages in their careers and those in leadership positions?

IS THIS GUY FOR REAL?

Shawn

Now in my third year of teaching, I have come to appreciate that my learning is not so different from [that of] the students I teach. We are as diverse as our students; we have different learning needs and different capacities to learn and develop. Just as my students are continually learning from my own experience and science expertise, there are many things I have yet to learn along my own career path, including, but not limited to, representing scientific activity for my students through their deep engagement in the practices of science.

My focus here is to address the conditions conducive to my professional learning as an early-career science teacher. Knowledgeable and passionate teachers need to be supported in their work. In my experience, important supports include the financial resources, departmental structures, collegiality, and learning beyond the school. These have all affected my own professional learning.

Financial Resources

As our principal slowly advanced toward our department head, I could see from the mutual disappointment in both their faces that the request for LCD projectors and iPads had been turned down. The best that could be offered was that "hopefully, we will have the money soon!"

The principal and chair knew, just as I did, that the projectors would have offered more resources for supporting student learning by giving students access to additional resources for constructing their own knowledge and supporting their engagement in authentic scenarios where they could practice applying scientific ideas and methods in novel contexts. I believe that having technology like this in a classroom environment, in combination with guidance and other instructional strategies, can do just that. Many websites and online instructional tools—for example, Spongelab, Edmodo, and BioGames—provide science resources where students are not relegated to repeating back what the teacher espouses; instead, in these environments they are able to inquire, obtain, interpret, evaluate, and synthesize and communicate information as they seek to answer questions—their own and others of societal importance. Being able to use these resources in the class would allow for modification of my own instruction over time to best accommodate reformed instructional approaches. Money, it seems, is always something of a barrier!

Departmental Structures

Despite monetary setbacks, there are resources that do not require funding at all (i.e., cooperation and collegiality). The desire for our science teachers to collaborate has proven valuable in my professional learning. Currently, our school has approximately 300 grade 9 students, and for a one-month unit each semester we collaborate to engage students authentically in work similar to that of scientists by ensuring that the practices of science are foregrounded to support students' development of defensible knowledge claims. This is something we also prioritize throughout the year, but having the chance to collaborate with all colleagues around this one-month unit is unique. The payoff in past years has been huge: The questions sparked in later units demonstrate students' interest in extending their knowledge about, and understanding of, the foundations of science itself. As a beginning teacher, having an entire department collaborate to shape and adhere to a similar teaching framework has helped modify my understanding of how to communicate these ideas to my students and reinforce the value that reformed teaching has for student learning.

Collegiality

"Perfect timing!" I thought. "Ms. Smith is sitting there eating lunch on the couch in the staff room, and I have been waiting to talk to her for the last week!" As I approached her, she greeted me with a cheerful hello. "Ms. Smith, could I talk to you for a second? I have an idea to integrate your biology lessons with some of my chemistry students …" Before I could even finish the question, her glistening smile and enthusiastic demeanor spoke for themselves. "Of course! It would be great to get our students working together! What did you have in mind?"

I was contemplating using a hip hop– and music-based instructional approach to science. You may be thinking, "Wow, is this guy actually serious? Hip hop in a science classroom?" The simple answer is yes, of course, anything is possible! Although the length of this vignette does not allow me to go into detail about this idea, just the ability to share and receive ideas with my colleagues has been quite enlightening!

Coordinating across departments and courses has provided a unique experience in which our teachers' knowledge is always exchanged to better accommodate the needs of our students. Thanks to multiple courses and the expertise of teachers across all departments, I have gained a better understanding of how I can support students to engage in the practices of science to apply and refine theoretical knowledge acquired in the classroom across multiple settings and contexts. It appears that the possibilities for cross-curricular activities and learning

initiatives are endless; that being said, my professional learning in this area has only just begun.

Beyond School Learning

Even though time is scarce, I make time to participate in my professional association. The annual Science Teachers' Association of Ontario conference provides numerous workshops that I believe help improve my teaching. The majority of workshops I attend focus on teachers sharing their expertise on various instructional approaches that promote the engagement of a range of students in authentic experiences where they use the practices of science to work on ideas for explaining the world around them. The hip hop in science idea mentioned previously was originally taken from this conference. Considering that most students in my class listen to the same music that I do and my desire to connect what we are learning with their interests, this was a perfect opportunity!

My role has changed only recently from being a student of science to being a teacher and student of science. In retrospect, both positions are the same, save for my responsibility to ensure that my students have an enjoyable experience and receive the best possible science education. Understanding how scientists and, subsequently, students can engage in the practices of science to develop rich understandings of the world is something that has been stressed extensively over the course of my own development, and with good reason. Engaging students in authentic disciplinary pursuits provides for an environment where students want to learn, inquire, and extend their own knowledge.

As a teacher, remaining open-minded, taking the initiative, being creative in my approach, and being willing to learn from others have paved the way for my personal and professional learning in science education. My own growth has largely been attributed to friends, colleagues, teachers, my own students, and professional opportunities. One thing has remained constant, though, and is the foundation for my growth as a science teacher: I have been and will continue to be a student of science through constant application of current and forthcoming scientific practices to afford my students the best possible experience through my own knowledge and expertise.

BUILDING A TEAM OF SCIENCE TEACHERS

Liz

One of my earliest memories of professional collaboration comes from the summer before I began teaching in my current district. Newly hired out of a school where I was one of two science teachers, I sat at a desk in a classroom with a handful of other teachers from the district. I remember that we were having serious conversations about how chemistry would be taught during the upcoming year. Having just finished my first year of teaching, I spent much of the time trying to determine when and how to voice my thoughts while also learning the dynamics of the other teachers in the room. Although this experience was slightly nerve-wracking, it set the stage for the importance that professional collaboration has within my school district and served to shape my professional learning both as a teacher and as an administrator.

Collaborative Planning Time
My school district prides itself on providing teachers with substantial time to work in collaborative teams both during the school year and in the summer. In addition to our summer curriculum time, teachers meet once a week for department meetings and are contractually guaranteed four full-day professional development days during the school year. Although teachers guide and ultimately complete the work that is done, the overarching direction of the work is determined by the department chairs at the two high schools within the district and is ultimately approved by our upper administrative team, which consists of assistant principals, principals, the assistant superintendent, and the superintendent.

The *NGSS (Next Generation Science Standards)* were recently adopted as the new state standards and will be fully implemented in the immediate future. To prepare teachers for the change in standards and—ultimately—teaching practices, my counterpart and I are focusing our attention in a few main directions. First, we knew that we would need to use the existing collaborative structure within the district of department meetings, institute days, and summer curriculum work. Second, we knew that we couldn't do all of the work ourselves and began looking for professional development (PD) opportunities for teachers, which are usually fully supported by the district. Finally, we focused on a strong level of professional trust that we have built between the science department and our upper administrative team.

Using Collaborative Structures

Department meetings are building a team of science teachers. This is a time to share informational items with our teachers, which is then often followed by time for departmental or content-related teamwork. As we prepare for the implementation of the *NGSS*, this time has become valuable for us to learn and collaborate together. Our initial conversations were centered on where the *NGSS* performance expectations (PEs) would fit into our sequence as a whole. Now we are working as content teams to develop and trial specific *NGSS* lessons.

In addition, we have approximately four professional development days during the school year (commonly known as "institute days"). Each day has a different focus as determined by the district, with different quantities of time for us to work as a department. Recently, departments have been given one full day, start to finish, that is entirely ours, as opposed to the few hours that we have typically been given. Having a full day has allowed us to be creative with our experiences for teachers, yet also specifically tailor days for them and their needs. One year, we brought in speakers to provide teachers with a crash-course experience in writing phenomenon-driven lessons; another year, we sent teachers to local schools that were in the process of implementing future initiatives of ours to see where they were in the process. Teachers have used this time to work collaboratively with those in the district to further their curriculum.

Initially, working on a team can be challenging, especially when different people have different viewpoints. Yet the strength of the teams within our district comes from the different perspectives that people bring to the team. To help make sure that everyone within our department and within the district were speaking a common language and shared a common level of understanding, we encouraged teachers to attend PD about the *NGSS*. Although some teachers were able to attend, others could not for a variety of reasons, and they received information during our weekly department meetings. This information was often presented by those who had attended trainings and felt comfortable with what they had learned. Teachers then put into practice what they had learned, shared, and decided on during their time with their collaborative team.

Finally, we have summer curriculum hours. To be paid for summer work, teachers and department chairs propose projects to the upper administrative team that are collaborated on by those within the district. Projects are approved on a variety of different criteria that shift from year to year as the focus of the district shifts. Typically, all areas that request time are awarded at least a portion of their requested hours. In the past, our requests have centered on the continued development of hands-on, inquiry-based investigations for our students. Recently, we have focused more on aligning our courses to the *NGSS* and, more specifically, designing phenomenon-driven experiences for students.

This past summer, our physics, chemistry, and biology teams met to take the *NGSS* PEs for their courses and place them together into potential units. Each content team made substantial progress. This work set the foundation for our work in the current academic year by continuing to build phenomenon-driven lessons and will serve as a starting place as we consider work for the upcoming summer.

In all of these experiences—department meetings, institute days, and summer curriculum work—teachers are expected to work as a team and eventually reach a consensus. As we continue to work to design research-based, phenomenon-driven lessons and experiences, our administrative team has supported us. All of our activities, from how our department meetings should be spent to the generous summer curriculum time allocation, have ultimately been approved by our administration. Our administrative team has trusted us to change and adapt as our standards have changed to better address how students learn science.

WE'RE TALKING ABOUT HOW SCIENCE IS DONE

Mike

I guess I'd start out by saying that much of my department's PD has come from within our departmental community. Certainly over the long haul, and where it concerns the teaching and learning of an accurate representation of science, the work of the department has evolved, becoming more sophisticated and making an impact on my professional practice.

There has been lots of externally sourced PD that has come and gone. Although much of it was useful, without the scaffolding offered by the department, it would have been difficult to sustain or grow.

In our science classes now, there really isn't a "teacher"—there's a learning community. We're way past having students memorize "the scientific method." In all our meetings, we're talking about how science is done. Students in my classes understand the need for a peer-reviewed methodology with a focus on conditions, variables, and trials as they work to support their claims. I was lucky that I was in the right place at the right time to slipstream in on the work that was done early in our board by teachers developing teacher and student awareness about the nature of science, scientific literacy, and the representation of science in the classroom—people like my chair and the veteran teachers I worked with in the early part of my career.

Departmental Collegiality

One strength of our department is our collegiality; we constantly feed off of each other. I can talk to anyone about reformed teaching and learning because we're speaking (and understanding) the same language. This is not by chance; we (the department) see great value in professionally developing preservice teachers and new members arriving in our school. Speaking personally, when I see young teachers come in and they really want to tackle inquiry and I see how excited they are for it, I find that I have so much to help them with, in terms of where I've had issues before or where I've had problems before. I guess my plowing through rough waters and making mistakes and learning from them has helped me guide new teachers when they come to our department. It's like, "OK, this really worked for me and this really helped me. This is where I ran into trouble." I have a feel for where kids can run into traps and where they might need some assistance, and I can offer those experiences to younger teachers. I don't think that there's a teacher in our department who has come in—not a single one—who's had a game-ending experience with inquiry. All of them have wanted to do it again and have found it tremendously successful, especially at the junior level.

Administrative Support and Reputation

A lot of professional research and documentation supported what we were trying to accomplish by focusing on inquiry, but because we had large numbers of students at all levels finding success with that approach, we also had tremendous support from our administration teams, who were able to see the evidence of student success for themselves.

Over the past 15 years, the department has developed such a solid reputation, and what it takes to go down that road, that others now take notice of us. We have many visitors from the science education profession come to observe our work and watch the students work. We also go on the road and talk about our experiences. Finally, we are being asked to develop and put on PD for others. Really what we are doing is sharing our own developmental experiences.

MODIFY IT AND RISK IT ALL AGAIN

Steve

I haven't had to rely on a lot of documentation supporting the teaching and learning of inquiry in science because of the collegiality of my department and the foundational strategies we have in place to support reformed teaching.

Taking Up a Chair's Challenge

We're a senior department now, but when we first came together (2001–2003), we were all roughly a decade into our careers. So we had some experience and enthusiasm and were ready to take on the challenge our chair was presenting to us, which was to start pursuing science education by using what was then called *scientific inquiry*. Two things developed out of that growth that helped make my career more enjoyable and the department more collegial. The first was that we started talking to each other far more than you might see in a more traditional setting. The reason was inquiry; we were always talking about what we were doing and learning. We were all learning and risking it together, in all courses, levels, and years, and we were building on a common platform. The other thing was that we began looking for connections between our subjects. By working with

a focus on inquiry, we began to find common ground between chemistry, biology, physics, and the Earth sciences, and that's something we see more and more often now in university, college, and private sector research.

Professional Learning Community

The department has developed as a professional learning community, which is not only useful to us but is also a great vehicle to help new or incoming teachers as well. It's amazing how many teachers new to our department would pick up on our approaches to teaching and learning. They would come into our department, we would help them pick it up, and they would put it into practice. It isn't just the old guard. Teachers arriving from other schools have always heard, "Oh, don't go to Churchill because of this and this," and then they get here and they love what we do. They find it very easy, straightforward. It's not a horror story. People get so frightened of changing practice, but when they got here, they put it into practice, and they love it. They look at our resources, what we're doing, learn with us, and then try to apply it and quite often meet with success. Sometimes they don't, but then they modify it and risk it all again.

THE RIGHT PEOPLE ON THE BUS

Julie

At the time of its publication, Jim Collins's book, *Good to Great: Why Some Companies Make the Leap … and Others Don't*, was viewed as an important piece of popular business literature. As part of our school's professional development for administrators and department chairs, my principal encouraged us to discuss this book at our weekly leadership meetings. One of Collins's premises is that we need to get the "right people on the bus" through the hiring process. In Collins's words, "The right people don't need to be tightly managed or fired up; they will be self-motivated by the inner drive to produce the best results and to be part of creating something great" (2001, p. 42). In our school, it's true for the teachers we hire and cultivate: Individuals may or may not have the specific skills and attitudes our department needs at first, but if they have the motivation, the ability to learn, and the interpersonal skills to work with others, they can help move our "bus" in the right direction.

Supportive Departmental Structures

Getting the "right people on the bus" is the easy part. Once on the bus, it's up to formal and informal leaders to create the structures that allow teachers to transform their passion for science education into results. These structures provide both the intellectual environment and organizational context for teacher learning. Providing teachers with strategically designed structures facilitates their natural dispositions to use their passion and interests in science education to reach our department goals. For several years now, our goal has been to improve our teaching of the practices of science, and this has required both high-quality teachers and supporting structures.

If the chair feels that the "right people" are not on the bus, well, frankly, not much can be done about that. What departments need from chairs are strategic leadership and the will to establish supporting structures in which all teachers, including those seemingly lacking the valued characteristics, might eventually reveal themselves as promoters of the department's goals. Supporting structures rely on chairs creating the conditions that promote change. Ely (1990) classified seven conditions that promote change: (1) dissatisfaction with the status quo, (2) participant knowledge and skills, (3) leadership, (4) rewards and incentives, (5) resources, (6) time, and (7) commitment. I see many of these conditions in the three main areas where I work best to facilitate teacher professional development: the relationship between the administration and teachers, information dissemination and analysis, and teacher collaboration.

Building Relationships and Trust

Teachers in our department understand the goals that we are working toward. Getting to this point, however, was not just a matter of making the announcement of "Hey, we're all teaching inquiry, so hop to it!" That has never worked and never will. An encouraging structure is built when chairs work with school administrators to lead instruction in their departments that contributes to meeting schoolwide goals. It is all about building relationships with administrators and their trust in the professionalism and creativity of the department. Mandates from administrators or outside experts are easily dismissed—"this too shall pass"—but initiatives explored by departments pique teachers' interest—"Hey, how does that work?"

Data-Directed Learning

Aligning the work of the department with schoolwide goals relies on information and the time to analyze and reflect on that information. Data about teaching and learning are key to catching our attention; it can be challenging to see enrollment data and to see how students feel about science and our classes. It was sharing data, combined with reading literature on reforms like the *National Science Education Standards* (NRC 1996) or the *NGSS*, that sparked our department's initial exploration of how we could enhance students' learning. And it is data that have kept our teachers identifying new areas of reform for us to investigate. Outside sources of expert information on science education—conferences, workshops, and graduate school—also help challenge the

status quo and build a supporting environment. In our department, we want people to ask questions when professional learning opportunities become available and then use those opportunities to develop answers. And the best way to develop answers is to work collaboratively.

Increasing teachers' understanding is greatly aided by collaboration—an essential component for supporting professional learning. Collaboration isn't as easy as it might sound—it is not just sharing. Collaboration is a recursive process of working together to accomplish a task. This requires actively listening, assembling information from various sources, being open to mistakes and brainstorming, reviewing products, refining work, and reflecting on progress. For some individuals, this comes naturally; for others, it can be challenging. In our department, collaboration is an expectation, from schoolwide committees to smaller content area teams. We want people on our bus who understand collaboration and have an openness to grow in their teaching. That also means we need infrastructure supportive of teacher learning.

Department Meetings

We already possess an infrastructure to support learning: department meetings. They can be filled with administrivia, or they can incorporate opportunities for collaboration. The best meetings materialize when I ask teachers to share what they have recently done in their classroom with their students, an idea they've been exploring with their content area team, the foundation of what they presented at a conference, or information they learned at a workshop. This is when I see the most passion, excitement, and intellectual curiosity displayed in department meetings—and this is what can light a fire with teachers.

When I ask teachers to share at department meetings, they first respond demurely, either out of modesty or intimidation. Fortunately, our department has experience with this practice of sharing during meetings, so we've discussed why we share and how difficult it can be to present in front of colleagues. If teachers know that the audience will be supportive, department meetings can be a great venue to provide a sharing teacher with implied or overt praise and recognition. This venue therefore not only propels our professional development academically but also provides the positive peer pressure and modeling that inspire others to learn more, explore new ideas, and take risks that might lead to them presenting and helping others grow.

Collaboration Time

Our school board understands that students benefit when teacher teams have the time to collaborate, plan curriculum, and reflect on student data. Our board has granted 14 "late-start days" each year during which teachers work in school, department, and content area teams in the morning before classes begin at 10 a.m. This becomes challenging, however, when schoolwide initiatives take time away from department projects. Strong personal and professional relationships between chairs and administrators are essential in dealing with these tensions. In addition to our late-start days, our board also provides funding for teacher teams to work on curriculum projects over the summer. This summer work is popular with our teachers, and teacher teams apply for funds every year. Although the hours awarded are almost always reduced from what had been requested and our science teachers know that they'll work more hours than what they are paid, they are happy that they get the nod of respect for the essential work they complete during the summer.

Moving toward our departmental goals took time, and it's still an ongoing process. Our department went through all of the stages of the change cycle, and growing pains still accompany us on our journey, especially as we work to implement the *NGSS*. However, strategic leadership efforts have softened the challenge, and knowing that we have board-provided infrastructure allows us to follow this path with security and confidence. Many specific leadership behaviors associated with change are discussed earlier in this book, but the foundation of these leadership strategies is the idea that educational leaders should provide the structure within which teachers can learn, create, collaborate, and reflect. This foundation is strengthened when you have "the right people on the bus" and when educational leaders understand their role(s) in arranging supporting structures.

Commentary on the Professional Learning Context

Our colleagues have shared their experiences of the contexts in which they work. These contexts vary in space from inner city to suburban to rural. They also vary in time, from 3 years in our profession to those approaching retirement after careers of more than 28 years. And yet ... there is a surprising constancy in their descriptions of the contexts that they see as crucial as supporting their professional learning. The words of our colleagues indicate that teachers *understand* how they can be best supported in their learning, regardless of their experience. They also give us powerful insights into the roles that teacher leaders have in *shaping* supportive contexts within and beyond their workplace. The words and emphases may vary, but the key messages are constant; supportive contexts are built over time, built on trusting relationships, and built deliberately with the support of administrators.

Time

Time—and how it is used—is an important factor in developing a supportive context. In considering time, our colleagues are clear. They need time to concentrate on what they consider important to their learning, even as the emphases of that learning change throughout their careers. Early in his career, Shawn needed time—indeed, he made time—to collaborate with his colleagues and his science teachers association. These collaborations, initially with trusted colleagues like Ms. Smith, were important to Shawn, as they gave him a chance to share, discuss, and develop ideas on teaching and learning with his colleagues. Over time, these collaborations have become more extensive and now include colleagues both throughout and outside his school. Liz, Mike, Steve, and Julie also recognize the importance of giving time and opportunities for new teachers to develop collaborative relationships. They recognize and understand the challenges that teachers face as they are "learning to find their voice" and have worked to build contexts in which teachers know "why we share and how difficult it can be to present in front of colleagues." For Mike, there is also a recognition of how he was helped by other teachers, being "in the right place at the right time." That recognition drives a commitment to be personally involved in "professionally developing preservice teachers and new members arriving in our school." Steve was adamant that teachers can reform their practices when they are properly supported:

> *People get so frightened of changing practice. ... They look at our*
> *resources, what we're doing, learn with us, and then try to apply it*
> *and quite often meet with success. Sometimes they don't, but then they*
> *modify it and risk it all again.*

All of the vignettes stress the importance of time in developing and maintaining collaborative relationships. However, the vignettes also show a changing emphasis on how time for professional learning is used. In the early stages of his career, Shawn needed time to share and discuss his ideas on teaching and learning. This is entirely understandable, but what is really interesting is that Shawn also recognized that this collaboration was within a departmental context built to "shape and adhere to a similar teaching framework." Mike's vignette reiterates this point over the 15 years he has been with his colleagues. The professional development that occurs within his department is the bedrock on which everything else is built. External expertise is important, but it is only sustainable if it aligns with the reforming orientation of the department. The key to this alignment is understanding the language of reforms, something that cannot be simply assumed: "I can talk to anyone about reformed teaching and learning because we're speaking (and understanding) the same language. This is not by chance. ..." Steve reiterated the same point: "We started talking to each other far more than you might see in a more traditional setting. ... We were building on a common platform. By working with the processes of science, we began to find common ground between [topics]." Julie is also clear in how time is critical in developing such a departmental context that supports professional learning: "Collaboration ... is not just sharing. Collaboration is a recursive process of working together to accomplish a task." Here is a recognition that time for professional learning needs to be prioritized while also balancing the professional learning needs of the department with those of all teachers, regardless of where they are in their careers. Goodrum, Hackling, and Rennie (2001) state the following:

> Teachers need to have time to develop ideas, reflect, discuss and be more collaborative. To assist teachers in this way, it will be necessary to acknowledge the importance of giving teachers time to think about their work ... relating to improved teacher knowledge and teaching strategies. (p. 91)

So how do we decide on the professional learning needs of the department? Mike spoke of the focus of their work with "a lot of professional research and documentation." In the same department, Steve spoke of being ready to "take on the challenge that our chair was presenting to us" even as he did not "rely on a lot of documentation ... because of the collegiality of the department." For both Julie and Liz as chairs, the implementation of the *NGSS* is the motivating force behind much of their departments' most recent professional learning experiences. The professional goals for these departments are coherent with the *NGSS* and therefore are also linked firmly to the prevailing discourse of science education. In Julie's department, the reform documents and data around teaching and learning—"seeing how students feel about science and our classes"—have shaped the professional learning goals of the department. Data on teaching and learning identify "new areas of reform for us to investigate" while a range of professional learning activities provide opportunities for "people to ask questions and then ... develop answers." In Liz's department, the chairs decide the overall direction of the professional learning, but it is linked to the implementation of the *NGSS*. Although the initial work was centered on performance expectations, opportunities have been developed that give teachers the responsibility to "guide and ultimately complete the work" in "content teams to develop and trial specific *NGSS* lessons."

Although the vignettes show the need to provide professional learning opportunities for teachers at all stages in their careers, they also highlight the need for those opportunities to be frequent. Each of our colleagues wrote of using department meetings as foundational opportunities for professional learning. To these opportunities were added days during the summer and days negotiated with administrators that could be devoted to activities deemed valuable to the teachers.

Time, as Shawn said, is scarce, so the frequency and variety of these opportunities reflect the importance of their frequency to the development of a supportive context. For our colleagues, however, the effective use of this time is predicated on relationships between teachers and administrators and the foundational virtue of trust.

Trust

When we argue that the vignettes show the need for trusting relationships, we are going beyond the personal relationships that people have in their workplace. We are also saying that the vignettes show that people need to have trust in the organizational processes of their institution. Experience has taught (and continues to teach) us a few important lessons around trust. Schools are highly political places; trust is slowly built over time but can be lost in the blink of an eye. What is fascinating in the vignettes is that our colleagues understand, and act on, the strong linkages between developing strong personal relationships and trust in organizational processes. Fullan (1992) has written about these linkages, stating that trust in organizational processes is a prerequisite for organizational growth and problem solving in a dynamic educational environment. The processes that need to be trusted are those that improve organizational "expertise and problem solving capacities [such as] improved communication, shared decision making, opportunities for collegial learning, networking outside the school environment, experimenting with new ideas and practices, commitment to continuous enquiry and so on" (p. 74).

From the early stages of their careers, Shawn, Liz, Mike, Julie, and Steve exemplify the dual nature of trust that we are looking at here, but how does it develop?

The trust that they have in their colleagues did not happen by chance. Shawn clearly established personal relationships with teachers such as Ms. Smith, which allowed him to choose the best time to talk to her about his ideas. The response from Ms. Smith only reinforces the need for teachers to develop personal relationships on which professional conversations can be built. For Liz, the first-year discussions on chemistry, although nerve-wracking, were also an opportunity to start learning "the dynamics of the other teachers in the room." Over time, understanding and developing empathy for the challenges involved in professional learning shaped Liz's "professional learning both as a teacher and as an administrator." Mike recognized his debt to the teachers he had worked with earlier in his career and now offers his experiences to new teachers: "I guess … making mistakes and learning from them has helped me guide new teachers when they come to our department." To offer guidance that shares both positive and negative experiences requires solid personal relationships built on trust. Steve recognized that for the reforms to continue, it couldn't be "just the old guard." As a department, they had a responsibility to share resources and practices in such a way that even if early attempts at reform were unsuccessful, then new teachers would "modify it and risk it all again."

The five vignettes highlight a reciprocity in taking responsibility for developing trusting relationships. For beginning teachers such as Shawn, there is a need to understand that being "willing to learn from others has paved the way for my personal and professional learning." Conversely, there is a responsibility on other teachers and teacher leaders to assist their colleagues in coming to this understanding. The building of strong personal and professional relationships is also foundational to developing trust in organizational processes. Shawn clearly made the educational case for the projectors and iPads to his chair and principal, and even though the decision went against him, he was prepared to accept it and move on. Mike trusted in the work of the department, knowing the work that had gone before, how the work was supported by the research literature, and, finally, the evidence of student success that he saw. Consequently, he expected support from the school administration "because they could see that student success evidence for themselves." Without an understanding of the people and processes involved in decision making, trust cannot develop.

Trust must also be nurtured, as both Liz and Julie understand. Julie sees her department meetings as crucial in supporting professional learning. Rather than "being filled with administrivia," the meetings are opportunities for sharing, discussing, and learning. The result is "passion, excitement, and intellectual curiosity." For Liz, the department meetings are "building a team of science teachers," but there is also a word of caution from both chairs. Building trust is a long-term proposition, but the benefits outweigh the costs, as Liz explains: "Initially, working on a team can be challenging, especially when different people have different viewpoints. Yet the strength of the teams within our district comes from the different perspectives that people bring to the team." Similarly, Julie recognizes that for some individuals, collaboration "comes naturally; for others, it can be challenging." Trust is built by engaging people in their own learning, which means that departments such as Julie's model "actively listening, assembling information from various sources, being open to mistakes and brainstorming, reviewing products, refining work, and reflecting on progress."

Liz's point about teachers having different viewpoints is an interesting one, as it highlights one of the qualities that Julie looks for when hiring teachers. To cultivate trust requires teachers to be more than content specialists. For Julie, teachers coming into the department must have "the motivation, the ability to learn, and the interpersonal skills to work with others." Recruiting may be the easy part; developing trust in one's colleagues and in the department is a long-term commitment. It is also only one part of the development of trust.

Departments do not exist in isolation from the rest of the school and wider education institutions. Being able to trust in the processes of these wider institutions is an exercise in reciprocity, giving all teachers and chairs a responsibility for engaging with the education world beyond their classroom. Make no mistake, there will be times when things go wrong, but those disappointments should not be seen as an excuse for not trying.

For beginning teachers like Shawn, with all the challenges that they face, engaging with colleagues throughout the school and with his professional organization is an excellent start. These opportunities already largely exist, but this requires taking the initiative to make the most of them and being prepared to learn from others' experiences. For experienced teachers like Mike and Steve, there is an openness and a certain pride in sharing the work of the department. This openness is reflected in welcoming visitors to their department, presenting at conferences, and being asked to present their experiences to other teachers within their own and other school boards. Mike also raises the important point that departments are different and that each one needs "to explore what [reforms] might look like for them." Or, as Steve saw it, reform did not need to be seen as a "horror story."

All departments are different, and part of that difference is the challenge of reconciling the professional learning needs of their teachers with the plethora of other demands made by school administrators, boards, curriculum reformers and professional developers, and legislators. As we shall discuss in the next section, working with administrators requires departments to be deliberate in their work and to develop personal relationships with administrators across schools and boards. As Julie notes: "Schoolwide initiatives take time away from department projects.

Strong personal and professional relationships between chairs and administrators are essential in dealing with these tensions."

Building Deliberately With the Support of Administrators

Even as we were writing this commentary, *NSTA Reports* (2016, p. 9) released the results of an anonymous poll on the support of administrators for hands-on science. Three numbers—and one comment—stood out in particular. Fifty-one percent of the respondents did not feel that school administrators support hands-on science. Seventy-eight percent of the respondents felt that administrators supported their professional development. Fifty-six percent of the respondents felt that administrators were "unwilling to learn more about subjects outside their own areas." The high level of administrative support for professional learning is encouraging, as it reflects an understanding that teacher learning is directly linked to student learning. In contrast, the negative perception of support for hands-on science and lack of scientific knowledge raises an interesting question: How do departments build the support of administrators? There is no single answer to this question, but the vignettes provide several useful pointers on how support can be built.

As chairs, Liz and Julie have already made it clear that developing strong personal relationships with administrators is important in building administrative support. Shawn's comment that he saw the chair and principal's "mutual disappointment" hints in the same direction. Mike made the comment that administration offered tremendous support because they could see that student success evidence for themselves. The implication is that the evidence has to be presented to the administration.

Strong personal relationships are foundational, but they will only get us so far. The strong professional relationships that are needed to build administrative support have to be based on a mutual understanding of *what* is important to science teachers and *why* it is important. Unless the administrators you are working with were once science teachers themselves (which can bring challenges of its own), then it is entirely reasonable that they would have a generic rather than complete understanding of the work of science teachers. Clearly—and the vignettes support this—we must work to bring administrators into our confidence and a deeper understanding of our work. As Julie puts it, administrators need to be able to "trust in the professionalism and creativity of the department." In each vignette, there appear to be two distinct parts to building this trust and the support of administrators for the work of science education.

The first is to understand and justify just what our own learning needs are. Professional learning gives teachers the capacity to question the practices of science for themselves and their department and from there develop new insights and practices that can be tested and validated in the context of classrooms with students. Huberman (1992) has described the trialing and questioning of ideas as "tinkering." Tinkering is the process through which teachers can take a good idea and develop it into "something worth subjecting to more systematic validation" (Hargreaves 2000, p. 231). In each of the vignettes, there is also an acceptance that outside expertise has a role to play in validating the professional learning of teachers. In validating our ideas, we clarify what is important to us and to our students. In Julie's vignette, this is best summarized by the following statement: "Teachers in our department understand the goals that we are working toward."

Shawn was adamant that data projectors could cater "to many of the unique learning needs of our students." The technology—and its uses—was grounded in an understanding of how it linked to a pedagogy of encouraging students to "inquire, interpret, and synthesize answers to questions." It was also linked to Shawn's desire to see a "modification of my own instruction over time." Mike was clear in what the department was trying to achieve: "We're way past having students memorize 'the scientific method.' In all our meetings, we're talking about how science is done." In his classroom, this translated into a focus on a more accurate representation of science: "the need for a peer-reviewed methodology with a focus on conditions, variables, and trials." Students see now that if the work isn't done with attention to these details, it won't pass scrutiny. For Liz, the planned adoption of the *NGSS* was the catalyst for starting to look at where "the performance expectations would fit into our sequence." From that beginning, teachers could then "develop and trial specific *NGSS* lessons." Julie's department is data driven, with enrollment trends and student perception data being used to spark "[the] department's initial exploration of how we could enhance students' learning" within the context of the school. Equally importantly, data are used to identify new areas for investigation. In each case, teachers, chairs, and departments are taking the responsibility for challenging the status quo and looking to improve the teaching and learning that occurs in their classrooms. Having teachers determine their professional learning needs is crucial. As Julie said: "Mandates from administrators or outside experts are easily dismissed—'this too shall pass'—but initiatives explored by departments pique teachers' interest—'Hey, how does that work?'" This commitment to taking responsibility for our own professional learning is foundational to communicating and building support for science education among administrators.

In the early stages of his career, Shawn did not talk explicitly about the links between the department and the school administration, but he understood the value of teaching with a common purpose—a purpose with which he felt comfortable. This meant that when an idea did not work out, he understood the reasoning behind the decision. As experienced teachers, Mike and Steve have taken on the responsibility of mentoring both beginning and preservice teachers. As a result of their departmental efforts, Mike said, "I don't think that there's a teacher in our department who's come in—not a single one—who's had a game-ending experience with inquiry." This is in a department in which it is the norm to see struggles as an opportunity to "modify it and risk it all again." Being successful in supporting teachers with reforms supports students in being successful. And evidence of student success is a valuable currency in the eyes of school administrators. As a chair, Julie sees the need to link the work of the department to the work of the school and actively works to build strategic relationships between teachers and administrators. The net result is that support exists for the professionalism of the teachers in the form of access to external professional learning opportunities and dedicated time to "collaborate, plan curriculum, and reflect on student data." Similarly, as they prepared to implement the *NGSS*, Liz's teachers understood that they "couldn't do all of the work [themselves] and began looking for professional development opportunities for teachers, which are usually fully supported by the district." Such a preparedness to ask for support was not seen as a weakness, for it was founded on the "strong level of professional trust that we have built between the science department and our upper administrative team." The support of the administration was built by constantly communicating the work of the department back to the administration: The result has been that the administration trusts "us to change and adapt as our standards have changed to better address how students learn science." In Julie's department, they are "happy that they get the nod of respect for the essential work they complete."

Conclusion

Changing the context of a department to one that supports professional learning requires work at many levels but is underpinned by a desire to take responsibility for improving teaching and learning for both teachers and students. All five vignettes highlight that teacher professional learning is much more than learning new content—it is about learning how to work together to develop a common language and philosophy of what reforms look like within the department while concurrently working to give that language and philosophy life in the classroom. Learning to work together requires time to cultivate the trusting relationships that support the challenges of questioning existing practice and developing reformed strategies for teaching and learning. It involves taking risks in teaching and learning and being prepared to try and try again in the face of failure. And it involves communicating our work to administrators and building their support for a reformed vision of science education.

4

The context in which you work will always be dynamic and will also need to be tended and nurtured. Developing the context, however, is foundational to working with the content of professional learning, which is what we discuss in the next chapter.

Summary

- Supportive contexts are built over time. Teachers need time to concentrate on what they consider important to their learning within their departments. Working with their colleagues allows teachers to learn from one another and to learn together.

- Supportive contexts are built on trust. This trust is rooted in the organizational processes of schools and districts. The trust that is built with colleagues doesn't happen by chance; instead, it is deliberately cultivated and sets the stage for collaborative professional learning.

- Supportive contexts are built deliberately with the support of administrators. Strong personal relationships are foundational, but they will only get us so far. The strong professional relationships that are needed to build administrative support have to be based on a mutual understanding of *what* is important to science teachers and *why* it is important. Teachers and departments must work to bring administrators into their confidence and develop a deeper understanding of their work as a science department and as science teachers. In the end, administrators need to be able to trust in the professionalism and creativity of the department.

Questions to Consider

1. To what extent do you feel sufficient time is built into your day-to-day schedule for collaboration and learning with colleagues?

2. What are possible ways that you can envision negotiating additional time within existing structures to allow for collaboration with other teachers in your department?

3. What are possible alternative ways of using time in your school or district that would support additional collaborative time with colleagues in your department? Remember to take into account existing limitations on administrators in terms of resources and scheduling.

4. To what extent do teachers within the department have trust in organizational processes? If this is not where you feel it needs to be, what

are potential ways in which the department might collectively seek to strengthen departmental trust in organizational processes, and how might this be negotiated in a nonthreatening way?

5. What are ways in which trust is deliberately built with colleagues in your department?

6. Are there additional deliberate methods that might be used to build trust and set the stage for collaborative professional learning?

7. How would you characterize your administrators' level of support? Are there opportunities to further bring administrators into your confidence as science teachers, and as a department, so that your administrators might more deeply understand your work?

8. What actions can you take as science teachers, or as a department, that would further support administrators in trusting in the professionalism and creativity of the department?

The Content of Professional Learning

The content of professional learning opportunities is an important consideration for science teachers, but the reforms of *A Framework for K–12 Science Education* (the *Framework*) and the *Next Generation Science Standards* (*NGSS*) mean that there is a change in emphasis for that content. As Reiser (2013) states, the reforms require that teachers

> help students continually work toward explanatory models, developing
> these ideas from evidence. This focus … challenges … teachers in how to
> motivate lessons through phenomena that need to be explained, how to
> help learners develop these explanations, and tie them to the phenomena
> and questions that motivated them. (p. 4)

What does this changing emphasis look like in departments that have been active in reforming teaching and learning? In Jason's experience:

> Over two years we invested a lot of time and energy into redefining
> what learning looks like in our classrooms. We focused on learning
> goals, established what it meant for students to be successful, and what
> types of feedback we should give our students. For many teachers it was
> a quantum leap from where they were already teaching.

In this chapter, our colleagues highlight how their relationship with content is evolving in response to the new and exciting challenges connected to recent reform. In considering their vignettes, we can see how that evolution changes over the course of a career.

5

A "STUDENT OF SCIENCE AND OF EDUCATION"

Shawn

Just as our current and future students learn from us, we must continue to evolve our own teaching and learning; one of the bases for this evolution is the information we learn and how it can be applied. In this vignette, I would like to address the content that has been conducive to my own professional learning and explain how this content has allowed me to extend my pedagogical knowledge.

The Disciplinary Knowledge of Science

Scientific content knowledge—or disciplinary core ideas—is an essential component of our teaching. As a young teacher of science, I have come to appreciate the grasp of knowledge I have and also be humbled by the knowledge I have not yet grasped as thoroughly as I'd like. This acknowledgment emphasizes the need to learn and incorporate new knowledge into my repertoire, in turn broadening students' understanding of scientific ideas and the practices of science. A strong and broad understanding of science allows me to engage directly with students in understanding more refined ideas. Most of us are specialists in at least one branch of science; however, increasing our knowledge across all sciences can prove to be useful when helping students make the connections between the major concepts of the disciplines and the knowledge expectations of the curriculum.

My professional learning of content knowledge has been an essential component to improving and expanding my existing teaching strategies. As students and teachers of science, our increasing knowledge can, in many respects, be gradually incorporated into our existing materials and teaching methods. A richer understanding of the practices of science also allows us to reconsider aspects of our teaching strategies. Understandably, this may increase the demands on teachers to further their knowledge in certain fields of science, even in the context of many teachers' family commitments, extracurriculars, or other time restrictions. However, from what I have experienced in my career so far, even the smallest pieces of knowledge we acquire can enhance our ability to support students in understanding concepts or disciplinary core ideas in science.

Considering How Students Learn

To teach content, we must be attentive to how our students learn, how we communicate concepts or ideas, and how we assess learning. The basics of my awareness of these ideas came directly from my teacher education training; teaching science from reformed perspectives and assessment strategies was an area I was familiar with but not practically experienced in before I obtained my bachelor's degree in education. Although earning this degree meant learning a combination of theoretical and practical applications, the emphasis was more on pedagogy. As my career has developed, there has been a shift from this emphasis to a more practical style of professional learning. Although additional qualification courses and workshops are an excellent source of information about student learning and assessment, I have found so far that colleagues and students are the best source of information in these areas. Who better to ask than the students who are learning from your teaching! Of course, the underlying pedagogy and theory must still be emphasized when taking colleagues' and students' opinions into account, but the prior experience of colleagues and the direct experience of students provide an excellent account of your teaching, especially in terms of how it can be modified to best accommodate student learning and how this learning is assessed.

Integrating Practice and Theory

Just as we can listen and learn from students and colleagues about how students learn, we may never discover if these ideas hold true if we do not desire to experiment with them. The majority of professional development workshops I have attended so far have provided theory on how best to approach different subjects and specific topics within those subjects; these ideas are always supported with practical exercises. These workshops, usually carried out by experienced teachers, have been incredibly informative and useful! I must stress from previous experience that a balance of theory and practice is critical in our growth as effective

science educators. However, a question may arise from this statement: Does this balance lie more toward theory or practice? Unfortunately, this is not a black-and-white question; I can say, however, that a balance should be established that works best for the students you have! And that balance is always going to be shifting as you gain more experience.

One of the most important ideas I adhere to is that we will always be students of science and of education no matter how experienced we become; there is always something to learn from both disciplines. As educators, we work with students, teachers, administrators, and parents to assist with student aspirations and accomplishments of learning and life goals. Similarly, we must aspire to learn and strive to further our own expertise as science educators. These aspirations come in light of the disciplines that we love; from my own experience, the content most conducive to my professional development comes directly from the colleagues and students I work with and from my motivation and drive to acquire knowledge. Students and colleagues have proven to be some of the most valuable resources for expanding my foundation in teaching the content and practices of science in understanding how students learn and how to integrate the theoretical and practical aspects of teaching. There will always be great students and teachers to learn from, and I also believe that I will be a lifelong learner in education and science; as a result, I can safely say that my professional learning will continue indefinitely!

EXPERIENCE THE MATERIAL

Liz

Throughout my experience as an educator and leader, I have participated in a considerable number of professional learning experiences. Some of these have been outstanding, whereas others have left a lot to be desired. When I reflect on these experiences, I find that authentic and discipline-specific professional learning, which forces me to experience the material in a similar manner to which I will use it in the classroom, has been the most beneficial.

Modeling Authentic Engagement

Shortly after the *NGSS* were released to the public but before my state had adopted them, a local university offered a summer course called "Teaching K–12 Science With the *NGSS*." I jumped at the chance to take this course for a number of different reasons. The *Framework* had been out for some time and although I knew it was important to read this prior to beginning work with the *NGSS*, I struggled to find the time to make it a priority during the school year. In addition, I knew that in my role as a department chair I would need to have a greater understanding of the *NGSS*. I would not only need to know about my area of expertise; I would need to know about additional disciplinary core ideas and their corresponding performance expectations, both within and leading into high school. This course seemed like the perfect exposure and—more importantly for me—I would be forced to make the time to look at both the *Framework* and the *NGSS*.

Although I expected the course to review the *Framework* and the *NGSS* from a K–12 perspective, I did not expect the course to engage us (teachers) as learners in ways that represented how the standards documents envisioned us engaging with students. I assumed that we would be participating in a book study—reading, discussing, and reading some more. Although there was reading, the course exemplified best practices in science education; instead of lecture, we were drawn into discussions and experiences that highlighted the intricacies of the *NGSS*. We held in-depth discussions about modeling and what made an effective model. We tried to explain how smells moved around the room. We looked at syringes and tried to model what happened to the air molecules when we compressed the plunger. We discussed phenomena and why they are compelling and necessary when designing lessons. We discussed how phenomena could drive a lesson and how student-generated questions about the phenomena could lead to experiences that would help students learn not only content but also scientific practices and skills. Finally, we put everything that we learned into practice and tried to write a unit of instruction, anchored by phenomena and supported by questions and subsequent experiences.

This experience was enriching, eye-opening, frustrating, and, most importantly, engaging. I was forced to work with the *Framework* and the *NGSS* in a manner that ultimately gave me a greater understanding of their complexities. I was also provided with experiences that I could bring back to teachers within the science department and students in the classroom. Through this experience, I gained confidence in working with the *Framework* and the *NGSS* that I would not have gained had someone just told me what I needed to know.

Using Past Experiences

Participating in authentic and discipline-specific professional learning that models classroom instruction is something that I had completed earlier in my teaching career as my district transitioned to the Physics First model of teaching. Going to Physics First was a huge curricular shift for us as a team, and for many it was a huge pedagogical shift as well. Although labs existed in our courses, there were not many, and those that did exist were cookbook in nature, which would need to change with Physics First. In addition to shifting pedagogy, we were also going to need to place teachers into areas that they were not necessarily comfortable teaching. For the first few years, we would need a number of different teachers to teach outside their content areas as our students worked their way into our new normal. We had enough teachers who were certified to teach physics; however, their backgrounds were in other content areas.

In working to get the entire department to a similar understanding of the pedagogy and content with regard to these changes in physics, every science teacher in the district was supported to attend a weeklong training about the philosophy of Physics First. During this training, we worked through labs as if we were students. We set up equipment, looked at data, compared results, had discussions, and were given the confidence to go into a school year with a new series of courses. When we modified our chemistry curriculum the following year, our chemistry teachers already knew the physics curriculum thanks, in part, to this professional learning experience. Participating in the program and knowing how our students were learning physics gave our chemistry team a strong foundation from which to build the chemistry curriculum.

Having been through a large curricular change and looking forward to a similar change with the implementation of the *NGSS*, we are looking to provide a similar professional learning experience for teachers. We brought in experts who have provided our teachers with authentic and discipline-specific learning experiences that exemplify the *NGSS*. We are sending teachers to conferences and professional development workshops where they can work with the *NGSS* and the *Framework*. We are providing teachers with time to understand the intricacies of a shifting pedagogical approach to science. Teachers have embraced the deliberate introduction to the *NGSS*, having seen the positive effects of successful professional learning in their classrooms not too long ago.

THIS LOOKS VERY DIFFERENT FOR ME TODAY

Mike

As I was cleaning up and organizing files and exemplars at the end of the last term, I came across some student inquiry products from more than 10 years ago. I thought to myself that I was holding some pretty good work but that today, in many respects, it didn't cut the mustard in terms of my current understanding of how to develop the process, product, and communicative skills about inquiry in the students—and their ability to apply that learning to producing a superior product.

Reform as Content

In my opinion, curriculum reform has been evolving from a time when importance was placed on what units will be in a course and the content that will be taught in those units to asking how students learn and how they can take control of their learning to maximize success. Beginning in grade 9, our department engages students with an accurate representation of science. Starting early gives us time to address the knowledge and practices in each unit and connect the two together as our students move through high school.

When you start teaching science with grade 9, you're teaching it in pieces, and often we have to relearn these pieces. Actually teaching what goes into a scientific report, helping students understand why that report is being written, and teaching students how to write is pretty daunting. If you can do that in little pieces, without them even realizing that they're writing a report, success follows. I have a lot of really cool things now developed as little pieces: how to teach students to develop a data set; how to teach students to write up an introduction to a lab; how to teach research; how to teach students to write a discussion, conclusions, and a hypothesis—all these are little pieces. I'm getting better now at putting those pieces together after 15 years of experience, learning from my mistakes, and reflecting with my colleagues. I also now share these things with younger teachers.

Focusing on Assessment and Evaluation

Although the heart of my professional development lies with the department, external expertise can have a significant impact. One initiative from the Ontario Ministry of Education and my board was professional learning in assessment and evaluation (A&E). The A&E initiative, combined with our work on inquiry, opened my eyes to the idea that assessment can be multifaceted, varied, and ongoing. That has had a major, ongoing impact on my practice, which is really something, considering that I'm in the last quarter of my teaching career. The major impact has been in terms of student success and my planning and delivery of lessons and assessments. As I worked with teachers and students, the initiative developed my ability to identify and communicate the success criteria necessary to guide the production of high-quality work and products.

Initially I was skeptical going into the work—"OK, here we go again." I was busy and remember being told that I was going to be on the A&E team. That probably ended up being the best thing for me, and my teaching, that I've done in years. It was exciting to have that happen toward the end of my career. One of the biggest impacts was my realization of how A&E can be used to support and strengthen a more accurate representation of science in the classroom. This was made clear by our professional development trainer from the Ministry of Education. He would tell our team that all of us learn best when we're doing and that we get better at it with practice. If I'm up in the front teaching, then I'm the one who's "doing science," and they're sitting there listening but not "doing science." We try to engage with our students as much as we can and have them carry out the little pieces of what we're teaching them. That's what makes the strategy different from being "hands on." For example, having students get together in a group and brainstorm several variables that you think might affect "the breathing rate of a fish" and then report back and discuss that with the class means that they are "doing science" rather than me telling them—the latter of which allows them to opt out of the thinking and learning. It's motivational, too, because the students are directing the conversation and engaging with scientific ideas and practices.

Learning and practicing more discipline-appropriate A&E strategies means that I can meaningfully assess a student's ability to communicate, observe, use critical thinking skills and understanding, self-assess, peer-assess, and give feedback. It's no longer just about performance on a test, exam, or product. All of this evidence allows me to sit back, reflect, and use the term *professional judgment* in a relevant way to come up with a final mark. It's now been a while since I have used software like Marks Manager as an accounting tool to crunch only the product or test data and come up with a student's average. For me now, if a student is sitting with a classmate having a conversation that is helping that other student come to a good understanding about a scientific idea or practice, then I have evidence that the student tutoring has mastered that scientific idea or practice. If I have another student who has developed a simple class resource package on how to negotiate Excel to generate a scatter plot, then I have evidence of his or her ability to graph as a sensemaking practice and am not limited by a small mistake that the student might make on a graphing test that ends up having a large impact on the overall mark.

The new knowledge I have about A&E has dovetailed with my inquiry understandings to increase student success. It all comes down to the question "What does a really good representation of science look like?" That's what I had to understand before I could improve my practice. Once you get that, you can also get at what constitutes success in each of the little pieces and how you assess and/or evaluate them. Once the students know what it is that they're attempting to do, they can start to coach each other. They should all have an understanding of what each of those little pieces should look like. In the real world, as in school, a lot of effective inquiry is done in teams. They'll divvy up the jobs and get to work. Back in the day, students would just put together the report they thought the teacher wanted, staple it, and hand it in. This looks very different for me today.

I'M A BIT OF A DINOSAUR, BUT I'VE LEARNED

Steve

Process is a big deal for me—not only those processes students go through to understand how science is carried out, but the processes that students use to manage their learning in the first place.

Colleagues Leading on Assessment

One of the major professional learning initiatives for our department has been the Ontario Ministry of Education's work on A&E, which Mike has already talked about. I wasn't selected to be part of the teacher teams, but because our department meetings provided opportunities for those who were involved to report back and discuss what they had learned, I was able to understand what was being conveyed and start to make changes to my practice. I think it's great that we have that communication. That's where I learned the content of the reform from, and then I followed up by talking to Mike on the side. Depending on the department, I believe it may not be necessary to take training sessions. If you've got a good, collegial department, the support structures, and teachers that are interested, then you have everybody on board and they're going to put in the effort. I think our department's been very, very good like that.

With the reforms to assessment, my initial thought was that this was a wonderful thing, especially as it allowed us to assess the practices of science across our subjects. So let's bring it into our classrooms and make the move from a predominance of summative assessments to a wide variety of formative assessments. I know that in my classes I never used to do that (formative assessment) too much, but I have started to do more over the last six years. Although the reform focused on assessment, in practice it also means working with students to get them to help each other, especially with descriptive feedback practices. It's important that these types of assessment take place before any testing or other summative practice. Students could have been working on an important assessment for a month and been totally lost. They hand in something that is unrelated to what you asked them to do. It's much more powerful for me and my students, when introducing practices such as argumentation, to do two formative assessments that don't end up getting a mark. Instead, there's an interview where I can give them descriptive feedback on where the work is headed and where questions can be clarified for both the students and myself. I'm a bit of a dinosaur, but I've learned.

AN APPRECIATION OF BOTH REAL SCIENCE *AND* REAL TEACHING

Julie

Learning styles were a cornerstone of teacher education when I began my teacher training in the mid-1990s. My previous academic pursuits had focused on scientific research, and my naïve mindset was that my own preferred way of learning worked really well. Discovering information about different learning styles and personality traits was one of the first times it struck me that not everyone liked the same approaches to learning that I did, and that my job as a teacher was not to change how students best learned but to work with these differences to help all students engage with and integrate new learning experiences. Although learning styles–based approaches have since come under increasing scrutiny (e.g., Pashler et al. 2008), understanding the diversity of learners' personalities was an important event for me as I moved from being surrounded by research-lab scientists to working with students and colleagues in K–12 educational systems.

The Unique Needs of Those Involved

Occasionally, when I work with teachers in other schools, my mindset can temporarily slip back into assuming that my audience enjoys the same approaches to learning as I do. Experience, however, has taught me that my consultations are most effective when I cater to a wider range of participants' proclivities. For instance, although most teachers in my own department enjoy learning about the underlying theory and empirical research base of a new educational method, other audiences may find the theory and research less important to their implementation of the work itself. Similarly, some audiences respond positively when I use more experiential learning strategies during professional development programs, whereas others prefer that I simply "get to the information." Appreciating audiences' varying comfort levels with different forms of presentation reinforces my understanding that my reflections on my own professional development preferences are bounded by my own experiences; therefore, what works for me and the teachers I interact with may not be the right approach for all science teachers.

Presenters are usually passionate about their subjects. Such passion often reveals a well-rounded understanding of a topic but other times can be experienced by attendees as a zeal that alienates other perspectives. From my experience as a teacher and educational leader, professional development must allow room for teachers' creativity, educational philosophies, and judgment of their students' interests and needs. Presenters are most effective when they understand that in order for teachers to embrace a new idea for their classrooms, they must be convinced of its likely effectiveness and its suitability for their idiomatic teaching approaches.

One of the many laudable aspects of teaching is that there is no "one" right way to do it; although there are globally effective strategies, sometimes what works for one teacher may not work for another. I think this is reflected in how teachers integrate reforms into their curriculum. There is a risk with dogmatic presentations on reform, which, although impassioned and possibly persuasive, can imply a lack of respect for the audience's knowledge and professionalism. For some audiences, this may be fine, but for others, a one-size-only approach to reform might ferment resistance where it doesn't need to be. When reforms are presented as flexible and adjustable approaches to science education, this lets them jive with current curricula, teacher skills, and student needs—it allows

teachers to more easily see how the reform could work for them and their students.

The Content Is Most Important

I frequently attend workshops and conferences with teachers from my department, often seeking sessions on approaches to the teaching and assessment of the practices of science. Our comfort with the presenters' approach to professional development is important, but it is the content of their presentations that most influences us. Content that moves us toward implementing the practices and their assessment in our own classrooms usually involves instruction that includes an appreciation of both real science and real teaching. It also involves an openness to teachers adapting reformed ideas that match their comfort levels as well as their students' interests and needs.

Coupling an adaptable approach to the practices of science with a strong understanding of the nature of science increases the effectiveness of professional development offerings. Understanding science content fully and deeply, making the connections from one content area to another, seeing the possible lines of investigation: This level of engagement in science is what we want for our students, but it is also what we want for ourselves. Immersing ourselves in science content gives us the flexible foundation that broadens our conceptualization of science and expands how we can portray and explore the practices of science in our classrooms. Having a strong and continually reinforced science content base increases our ability to create lessons and laboratory experiences for our students and helps us problem solve as we inquire side by side with our students. Science content helps scientists as they conduct experiments, and it helps teachers as they create experiences that convey scientific ideas and processes to their students.

Grounded in Classroom Implementation

The final ingredient that I think increases the effectiveness of a presentation on reforms is an understanding of the real-world classroom. One of the most frustrating experiences for my teachers is sitting through a presentation by someone who has an intriguing idea that would be interesting to consider in an idealized world but that appears unworkable within the constraints of a normal classroom setting. Presenters who are aware of teachers' day-to-day work are also likely to understand that teachers lack the flexibility or the control to cut massive amounts of content from their curriculum. Reform projects that require six weeks to complete might work if they are carefully crafted to integrate with required course content; however, if they simply add six extra weeks of classwork, then teachers will struggle (or, more accurately, won't bother) to identify which of their existing lessons and activities to correspondingly remove.

This is especially true if teachers work on a team in which a single teacher has to persuade team members to try something new. If new instructional and assessment strategies fit with the team's philosophies and do not require the removal of key units of work that are valued by the team, then the task is not as difficult as it would be to persuade a team to cut an entire unit. Practices that can be incorporated into teachers' existing curricula have a much better chance of success than reform that requires a large, immediate curricular overhaul. The beauty of incorporating reforms into the curriculum in "half-steps" is that as teachers experience success and attempt more small moves toward the ideal of the reform, these steps can accrue into substantial change over time.

Reflecting on how professional development best enhances teachers' growth and subsequent teaching, I think that the fit between the participants and the presentation is key. "Knowing their audience," effective presenters not only accommodate teachers' prior knowledge, confidence levels, and motivations but also listen sensitively to understand teachers' school structures and the needs of their specific student populations. I also think teachers are most receptive to content when it is presented with an openness to incremental adaptations. Finally, for my own department, professional development that affirms both of the fields we are immersed in—education and science—is critical. Science teachers like science—actually, we love science. The ongoing question that we work to answer through our experiences and our continued professional development is how we can best get students in our classrooms to understand, use, and love science, too.

Commentary on the Content of Professional Learning

If it ever was, science teaching can no longer be about the presentation of decontextualized, immutable "facts." The reforms of the past two decades have consistently stressed the need for teachers to develop classrooms in which students work to shape ideas from evidence that explain the *why* and *how* of natural phenomena. As a result, the content of professional learning opportunities must be more than disciplinary knowledge; it must also include how to use that knowledge in a way that reflects the human construct that is science. Each of our colleagues' vignettes reflects this wider understanding of content: a broader and deeper understanding of disciplinary knowledge (from science and education), the integration of theory and practice, and an understanding of how students learn.

Broader and Deeper Disciplinary Knowledge

Regardless of their years teaching, all of our colleagues spoke of a need to learn more about both science and education. In science, there was a need to learn disciplinary knowledge, not just in the specific topic area but also across the discipline and the practices that bind the topics together. This learning was not restricted to just the latest developments in the discipline but instead led to a richer understanding of the discipline and how it came to be. In education, there was a recognition of needing to learn how students learn, how to assess student work, and how to develop credible teaching strategies for the learning required by the reforms. As Shawn said, teachers need to simultaneously be "students of science and of education, no matter how experienced we become."

Science content knowledge is the foundation on which our work is based. Usually educated and certified as specialists in particular science topics, we are often called on to teach across the discipline. This can be daunting for beginning teachers, as it leaves us more confident in some topics than others. Having a "strong and broad understanding of science" allowed Shawn "to engage directly with students in understanding more refined scientific ideas." Developing our content knowledge builds confidence across and between topics, "helping students make the connections between major concepts and the knowledge expectations of the curriculum." For Mike, there was a desire to work as a department to "address the knowledge and practices in each unit and connect the two together as our students move through high school." Steve believed that the changes in assessment were beneficial in developing the practices of science across the topics that he taught. Julie, with an equal wealth of experience, reiterated the same point. For her, making connections between topics gives teachers and students the opportunity to develop "possible lines of investigation" and build the level of engagement in science that "we want for our students [but also] what we want for ourselves." As a teacher and chair, Liz expanded on the importance of content knowledge in her own specialization and "additional disciplinary core ideas" to the need to be aware of what to expect from students coming into high school science from elementary schools. This is an essential point, as reform documents such as the *Framework* and the *NGSS* discuss science education being a continuum from K to 12, and we ignore that continuum at our own risk. Education is a continuum, and teachers need to be cognizant of the knowledge students are bringing into the classroom. The disciplinary core ideas are also central to the other side of content knowledge—the practices that shape the scientific enterprise.

For Julie, content must be seen in its broadest sense: "Science content gives us the flexible foundation that broadens our conceptualization of science and expands how we can portray and explore the practices of science in our classrooms." The building of a "flexible foundation" can also act as a motivator for challenging existing teaching practices, as Shawn noted: "A richer understanding of the practices of science also allows us to reconsider aspects of our teaching strategies." Mike spoke of teaching in "pieces" and helping students understand—and have opportunities to practice—those pieces. By understanding the "pieces" himself, Mike was then in a position to help his students understand what success in "each of those little pieces should look like." By teaching science content and practices as "little pieces," Mike has moved his students beyond the point where "students would just put together the report they thought the teacher wanted, staple it, and hand it in." Similarly, Steve used the assessment reforms to help his students improve their understanding of the practices of science. Rather than allowing students to be "totally lost," the use of formative assessments allows for the provision of "descriptive feedback on where the work is headed and questions [that] can be clarified for both the students and [teachers]."

Understanding and constantly reinforcing the practices of science allows teachers to move beyond the transmission of science "facts" to the ability to "create lessons and laboratory experiences for our students and [to] problem solve as we inquire side by side with our students." In this nutshell, Julie has encapsulated the reforms promoted by the *Framework* and the *NGSS*.

Although we may pursue a broader and deeper understanding of science, we also need to move toward a greater alignment of our teaching practices toward the ideals of the reform documents. This means constantly evolving our understanding of teaching and learning. Even in the early stages of his career, Shawn was already noticing changes in how he was approaching the task of learning more about education. Moving away from the focus on pedagogy in his teacher education program, he was now focusing his learning on the areas of greatest importance to him: "how our students learn, how we communicate concepts, and how

The Content of Professional Learning

we assess learning." His preservice education gave him a familiarity with reformed perspectives on teaching, but not with the practical experience of teaching. Now as his career has developed, he is pursuing "a more practical style of professional learning," relying on additional qualification courses and workshops on student learning and assessment and working on weaving the "underlying pedagogy and theory" into his work with students and colleagues.

For Liz and her colleagues, the introduction of the Physics First model of teaching helped reveal similar issues of needing to be specific in focusing their professional learning on the needs of a particular reform. In her case, there was a recognition that professional learning needed to simultaneously focus on both content and pedagogy. There was a need to reimagine the way in which physics had been taught, leading to a common departmental understanding of the pedagogy and content of the new program. Developing this common understanding meant, for example, that the labs "that did exist were cookbook in nature, which would need to change with Physics First." Such an approach was invaluable, as a number of teachers "were not necessarily comfortable teaching … outside their content areas." The concentration on working with both the content and the pedagogy required for the Physics First program has given the department confidence in how it can approach the implementation of the *NGSS:* "We brought in experts [and now send] teachers to conferences and professional development workshops."

Mike and Steve's teaching and learning of a reformed vision of science was heavily influenced by the work of their department. Mike was initially skeptical of being involved in the A&E professional development: "OK, here we go again." Two aspects of Mike's vignette are instructive for us. The first is that he made connections between his previous professional learning and the new information he was working with: "One of the biggest impacts was my realization of how A&E can be used to support and strengthen a more accurate representation of science in the classroom." Such an openness to learning allowed Mike to understand *what* aspects of his practice needed to change, *why* they needed to change, and *how* to reform his teaching. All of this is encapsulated in the statement, "If I'm up in the front teaching, then I'm the one who's 'doing science,' and they're sitting there listening but not 'doing science,' … which allows them to opt out of the thinking and learning." The second important aspect of Mike's vignette is that the A&E professional development opportunity was discipline specific. Mike could take the content that was being offered and make use of it in his classroom: "I can meaningfully assess a student's ability to communicate, observe, use critical thinking skills and understandings, self-assess, peer-assess, and give feedback."

Steve was not part of the formal training, but working in a collegial department that made time to talk about practices and working closely with Mike "on the side" allowed Steve to experiment with the reforms in his classroom. Steve noted that communication was key to his learning about the reforms and that the communication needed to reach everybody to build interest in the reform. What is also interesting from Steve's vignette is that the assessment reforms built on the work that the department had already put into teaching the practices of science. Steve instantly saw the value of the assessment reforms: "This was a wonderful thing, especially as it allowed us to assess the practices of science across our subjects. So let's bring it into our classrooms and make the move." In turn, the assessment reforms led to further changes in Steve's classroom practice: "It also means working with students to get them to help each other, especially with descriptive feedback practices." This is an important point, as it highlights how reform is a gradual process and needs to be seen as evolutionary, not revolutionary. As in Liz's department, professional learning opportunities are at their most valuable when they involve teachers with authentic and discipline-specific learning experiences.

Julie learned an important lesson early in her career: "It struck me that not everyone liked the same approaches to learning that I did, and that my job as a teacher was not to change how students best learned but to work with these differences to help all students engage with and integrate new learning experiences." This understanding has shaped a strong commitment to professional learning that respects teachers as learners. In teaching, "there is no 'one' right way to do it; although there are globally effective strategies, sometimes what works for one teacher may not work for another. I think this is reflected in how teachers integrate reforms into their curriculum." This means that a key component in aligning our teaching practices with the ideals of reform documents is encouraging "teachers to more easily see how the reform could work for them and their students." For chairs and other teacher leaders, this means that professional learning in the department must achieve two functions. First, it must affirm both of the fields we are immersed in, education *and* science. Second, it must take into account teachers' prior knowledge, confidence levels, motivations, school structures, and the needs of their specific student populations. The achievement of these functions relies on working with content that helps us implement "the practices and their assessment in our own classrooms [and involves] an appreciation of both real science *and* real teaching. It also involves an openness to teachers adapting reformed ideas that match their comfort levels as well as their students' interests and needs." To successfully develop such professional learning opportunities requires the integration of both theory and practice, a point made by each of our colleagues.

Theory and Practice

Teachers' knowledge is both tacit and explicit, and both forms need to be developed through professional learning opportunities. Teachers are experts at generating tacit knowledge through their classroom work. This tacit knowledge can become explicit knowledge when teachers work with their colleagues and tell stories of practice and "what works." The capacity to tell stories makes "tacit knowledge more visible, call[s] into question assumptions about common practices … and make[s] possible the consideration of alternatives" (Cochran-Smith and Lytle 1999, p. 294). If we wish to develop teachers' knowledge, then we need to provide the conditions in which there is a "willingness to accept feedback and work toward improvement … respect and trust" (Hord 1997, p. 5). You may have already picked up on the dangers of leaving the responsibility for generating knowledge at a department, school, or even board level. The first is that telling stories of practice only provides information to another teacher; it does not provide knowledge. Second, the desire to tell stories must be fused with a desire to reflect on thoughts, words, and actions. And reflection can only be effective when alternatives become known and explored. In other words, theory and practice need to be two sides of the same coin.

Shawn recognizes just this point when he says that "we can listen and learn from students and colleagues about how students learn, [but] we may never discover if these ideas hold true if we do not desire to experiment with them." For Shawn, the mix of theory and practice is foundational to his learning: "The majority of professional development workshops … have provided a theory on how best to approach different subjects and specific topics within those subjects; these ideas are always supported with practical exercises. … a balance of theory and practice is critical in our growth as effective science educators." Where this balance between theory and practice lies, however, is problematic. For Shawn, in the early stages of his career, the motivating force in finding the balance is the needs of his students; the "balance should be established that works best for the students you have!" That is not a bad rule of thumb.

Liz's experience with the *NGSS* course encapsulates the need to integrate theory and practice: "Through this experience I gained a confidence in working with … [the] *NGSS* that I would not have gained had someone just told me what I needed to know." The strength of the course was that it went beyond making the theory known: "a book study—reading, discussing, and reading some more." Theory and practice were integrated to exemplify "best practices in science education; instead of lecture, we were drawn into discussions and experiences that highlighted the intricacies of the *NGSS*." The net result was "enriching, eye-opening, frustrating, and, most importantly, engaging. I was forced to work with … the *NGSS* in a manner that ultimately gave me a greater understanding of their complexities." And, as with Shawn, the integration of theory and practice was seen as benefiting the teachers and students in Liz's department: "I was also provided with experiences that I could bring back to teachers within the science department and students in the classroom."

The integration of theory and practice for Mike and Steve was much more specific, though no less valuable. Both were already well versed in teaching from a reformed perspective but also realized that their assessment practices had not evolved to align with their teaching. As Mike said, "I thought to myself that I was holding some pretty good work but that today, in many respects, it didn't cut the mustard in terms of my current understanding." For Steve, the benefit was in understanding more about the "processes that students use to manage their learning in the first place." The professional learning on assessment could be linked to his previous work on the practices of science, thus validating and amplifying the importance of his previous work: "It's much more powerful for me and my students when introducing processes such as argumentation." For Mike, the strength of the professional learning was that it involved working with a Ministry trainer, his colleagues, and his students to develop "[his] ability to identify and communicate the success criteria necessary to guide the production of high-quality work and products." The inclusion of students in this is interesting, as the student perspective is often ignored. Further, the focus was on assessing the different forms of evidence of learning that teachers can use rather than using "an accounting tool to crunch only the product or test data and come up with a student's average." By more closely integrating A&E with his reformed teaching practice, Mike has moved closer to more accurately representing science: "It's no longer just about performance on a test, exam, or product."

Julie's vignette brings a different perspective to this discussion. As an experienced chair and facilitator of professional learning opportunities, she highlights the variability in teachers' responses to the integration of theory and practice: "Although most teachers in my own department enjoy learning about the underlying theory and empirical research base of a new educational method, other audiences may find the theory and research less important to their implementation of the work itself." The challenge is to integrate theory and practice in ways that build the credibility of the reform. Teachers need to be "convinced of the likely effectiveness [of the reform] and its suitability for their idiomatic teaching approaches." The alternative is—well, we have all experienced this at some point in our careers—"dogmatic presentations on reform, which, although impassioned and possibly persuasive, can imply a lack of respect for the audience's knowledge and professionalism."

Understanding the relationships between theory and practice is crucial, as is the perceived credibility of the reform in the eyes of the teachers. Credibility can be built when the presentation of the reform is presented in a way that shows, in Julie's words, an "understanding of the real-world classroom" and how students learn in those classrooms. This is the final point that we wish to consider from these vignettes.

How Students Learn

As a beginning teacher, Shawn is clearly (almost idealistically) concerned with how his students learn and how he can learn from them: The "direct experience of students gives an excellent account of your teaching … how it can be modified to best accommodate student learning." This is an admirable position to take, as it appears to be a motivation for reflection on how Shawn can continue to improve this classroom practice "for expanding my foundation in teaching the content and processes of science … in understanding how students learn." Understanding how students learn is also important to Liz, as it gave her confidence in the professional learning that her teachers were undertaking as part of the Physics First and chemistry curriculum changes:

> We worked through labs as if we were students. We set up equipment, looked at data, compared results, had discussions, and were given the confidence to go into a school year with a new series of courses. … Participating in the program and knowing how our students were learning physics gave our chemistry team a strong foundation from which to build the chemistry curriculum.

This practical understanding of the professional learning requirements for particular reforms has been reinforced by other forms of professional learning such as collaboration with external experts and sending teachers to conferences.

Despite the apparent success of these professional learning opportunities, Liz implied that they are not the norm. Referring to the *NGSS* course, she says, "I did not expect the course to engage us (teachers) as learners in ways that represented how the standards documents envisioned us engaging with students." However, the content of the course reinforced the efficacy of understanding the content from a student perspective: "We discussed how phenomena could drive a lesson and how student-generated questions … would help students learn not only content but also scientific practices and skills."

Mike highlighted a long-term view of how student learning is changing, a change from discussing what "units will be in a course and the content that will be taught in those units to asking how students learn." This perception is based on the work—of more than 15 years—of his department in promoting a reformed vision of science education. For Mike and his colleagues, students learn by "doing science" rather than by passively listening. Mike's practice is to engage students with science and provide opportunities for them to work with both science content and practices. In addition, he is explicit in working with students to understand what success looks like for the work they are doing so that they know "what it is that they're attempting to do." He also relies on a range of evidence to make sure that learning is appropriately assessed or evaluated.

Not surprisingly, Steve shared a similar long-term view and is concerned with understanding "those processes students go through to understand how science is carried out [and] the processes that students use to manage their learning in the first place." Even as he was working to incorporate the practices of science into his teaching, he also started to look at how assessment needed to change. As a result, he was ahead of the assessment reforms, which have only been implemented in the last few years: "I know that in my classes I never used to do [formative assessment] too much, but I have started to do more over the last six years." Working with students in developing assessment tools has meant changing his perception of himself as a teacher as well. Working with the reforms sees Steve as a co-inquirer into the practices of science, something he takes a quiet pride in: "Questions can be clarified for both the students and myself. I'm a bit of a dinosaur, but I've learned."

Similarly, for Julie, students also learn by doing, where doing is based on a sophisticated understanding of science and with teachers as co-inquirers with their students. The motivation here is the same as what drives Shawn, although they are years apart in terms of experience. For Julie, students learn when they have opportunities for understanding content and making connections and can pursue their own lines of investigation: "This level of engagement in science is what we want for our students, but it is also what we want for ourselves." The creation of lessons and laboratory experiences opens up opportunities that allow teachers to "problem solve as we inquire side by side with our students."

Conclusion

What is interesting in this series of vignettes is that our colleagues identified and have experienced all of the components of the Timperley et al. (2007) framework regarding the content of professional learning opportunities. Occupying different stages in their careers or positions within their departments has made little difference to the main concerns that our colleagues have about the content component of their work. All were driven by a desire to understand how students learn and then use this information to reform their classroom practices to align with the ideals of the reform documents that they were working with. From this intrinsic motivation comes a need to develop both disciplinary and pedagogical knowledge as well as to integrate this knowledge back into their classroom practices.

To support this virtuous cycle of learning, external expertise is important in helping advise and guide the implementation of reforms. The real bedrock on which changes to classroom practice occur, however, is at the department level. In every vignette, the opportunities to discuss teaching and learning—either as a department or with particular colleagues—are seen as crucial to learning and applying new knowledge to the classroom. As such, the content and the context of teacher professional learning become almost indivisible. If we are to build departments that promote teacher professional learning, then we need to embed the content of the reforms into reforming the department. This idea is well understood in the research literature; we need to make it equally understood in departments. It is the professional learning activities that teachers engage in that can become the vehicles for making this connection and then bringing it to life. It is these activities to which we turn our attention in the next chapter.

Summary

- Science teaching can no longer be about the presentation of decontextualized, immutable "facts." The reforms of the past two decades have consistently stressed the need for teachers to develop classrooms in which students work to shape ideas from evidence that explain the *why* and *how* of natural phenomena. As a result, the content of professional learning opportunities must be more than disciplinary knowledge; it must also include how to use that knowledge in a way that reflects the human construct that is science.

- Although we may pursue a broader and deeper understanding of science, we also need to move toward a greater alignment of our teaching practices with the ideals of the reform documents. This means constantly evolving our understanding of teaching and learning.

- Professional learning in the department must achieve two functions. First, it must affirm both of the fields we are immersed in—education *and* science. Second, it must take into account teachers' prior knowledge, confidence levels, motivations, and school structures, as well as the needs of specific student populations.

- Understanding the relationships between theory and practice is crucial, as is the perceived credibility of the reform in the eyes of the teachers. Credibility can be built when reforms are seen as credible and address how students learn in classrooms.

- A focus on how students learn is centrally important when considering the content of professional learning.

- Opportunities to discuss teaching and learning—either as a department or with particular colleagues—are seen as crucial to learning and applying new knowledge to the classroom.

Questions to Consider

1. What are the ways you and your colleagues can support or have supported each other in building robust and flexible content knowledge? How might the dimensions of the *Framework* (i.e., Chapters 3–8) be used within the department to support this pursuit?

2. In what ways can teachers in schools and departments be supported to learn continuously as our knowledge from research about science teaching and learning evolves? What strategies might the department use to ensure that new developments related to science teaching and learning are understood and integrated into the evolving departmental visions of science education? (Consider mechanisms to support teachers' reading and sharing resources from National Science Teachers Association journals or ways to connect with science education leaders outside of the school.)

3. What mechanisms are in place, or could be put in place, to support the integration of what teachers are learning with the expertise and experiences they already have from their years of experience in classrooms?

4. To what extent do departmental or individual discussions center on student work as a mechanism for focusing professional learning on how students learn? When could opportunities for such discussions occur in the school or department?

5. How might the discussions about science teaching and learning in the school or department be enhanced to further support teacher professional learning?

The Activities That Promote Professional Learning

No single activity will promote teacher professional learning; rather, we know that activities need to be actively embedded in the subject matter, connected to teachers' extant practices, and coherent across the scope of reform documents. As Jason explains from his time in charge of a board professional learning program:

> We worked on subject-specific group planning, sharing and demonstrating new strategies, and consolidating our learning in conversations with our peers. The feedback I got was that in small groups that coplanned and cotaught, there was a lot of innovation and progress. All teachers felt it was the most productive professional learning they had done, many in their entire career.

By working with appropriate strategies at the appropriate time and in appropriate contexts, reform proposals can come to life as teachers are given opportunities to work with the activities and with their colleagues. The following vignettes highlight teachers' experiences with these activities at different points in their careers.

I CAN FOSTER KNOWLEDGE, INQUIRY, AND CREATIVITY

Shawn

As a student both in high school and at university, I remember many of the activities that promoted my interests in science. Most had a strong foundation in direct instruction of theory and a follow-up integration of theory into practice. One thing I found, however, is that many of these activities did not have as much of a creative or innovative approach to applying the concepts in question. Just as the instructions were direct, so was the narrow viewpoint of the integration of theory into the subsequent activity. Throughout my university experience, especially as a preservice teacher, the gears seemed to shift more toward direct instruction followed by an open and differentiated practical application. The knowledge I gained was not simply put into practice as per teacher instructions but rather as a guided inquiry and divergent discovery of ideas. As my experience has grown, I have come to appreciate how important this approach is both for my learning and for the learning of my students. Reflecting on prior educational experience as both a student and a teacher has also allowed me a deeper understanding of the effectiveness of different methods of communication in activities. However limited my professional development is as a new teacher, many activities have proven to be beneficial throughout my development over the last few years.

Learning From Colleagues

Before becoming a permanent member of my school board several years ago, I had no choice but to move from school to school through contract positions. These positions would allow for a temporary spot, usually a year or less, to cover the position of permanent teachers on maternity or medical leave. Although this was hard in terms of building a community and relationships with students, it did provide an excellent opportunity to learn from other science teachers. One program our board offers to new teachers is an induction program; recently hired teachers are paired with a teacher with at least five years of experience who shares his or her understanding of student learning and provides instructional materials that the recently hired teacher can use.

Many of the teachers I worked with, including the individual from the induction program, were willing to sit down and share their work and perspectives on how students learn best in science classrooms. They were also willing to constructively criticize my methods of instruction and communication through direct observation. Feedback was always welcome and although we may not have agreed on everything, it provided an opportunity for self-reflection along with the opportunity for integration of new practices into my existing repertoire. For example, something as simple as pointing out how a graphic organizer may work better in communicating chemical naming and classification gave me a better idea of how to effectively communicate concepts to my students. Although that is not the only method I use for supporting students in naming chemicals, I have taken the idea, modified it, and integrated it into my practice. By the same token, many science teachers have allowed me to watch their methods of teaching concepts in their classrooms; I found that direct observation in both respects, as the observer and the observed, has been invaluable in my growth as a science teacher. As time has passed, I have found that many of the ideas that were communicated to me and that I have observed since the induction program have worked their way into my teaching practices.

Building My Own Pedagogy

Given the myriad of different teaching styles and the willingness of colleagues to share their expertise, I was able to pull what I found most useful from each style and incorporate these aspects into my own pedagogy. Some of the simplest labs I received and subsequently modified provided excellent approaches to inquiry-based problems while addressing the most important aspects of labs in high school, such as Bunsen burner safety. One section of my lab instructs students to puncture a sewing pin through the head of a match at a 90° angle. The pinhead and match are then placed on top of the Bunsen burner; when the burner is lit, the match on the pinhead will not burn. A simple question that challenges student understanding is why—why would

something that is supposed to burn in the presence of a flame not burn at all? Before my colleagues would explain the theory behind the lab, they would encourage me to work through it myself to gain an understanding of how I would approach the problem and how I could guide students to inquire. I found that this approach of self-understanding in inquiry-based labs provided an opportunity to gear my thoughts toward how students may approach questions in that lab.

Learning From Others

My professional education has not been limited to learning from teachers within our school and board; some of the best instances of development have come from my participation in external sources of education. When working through my honor specializations in biology and chemistry, I had the opportunity to work with individuals from multiple school boards and with varying degrees of experience. Similarly, my training through the IB (International Baccalaureate) program for chemistry has been invaluable in understanding how I can foster knowledge, inquiry, and creativity in my students. Discussions including, but not limited to, re-evaluating the use and effectiveness of science textbooks, using predict–observe–explain methods to reinforce inquiry in lab activities and demos, addressing student misconceptions in biology and chemistry, and creating student-designed inquiry-based lab instructions have all provided an opportunity for self-reflection with respect to my teaching practices. The perspectives of colleagues and those of my professors have challenged some of my teaching strategies and positively reinforced others; in essence, these workshops have provided some of the best professional development activities throughout my career so far.

Reflecting on my own learning since the start of my professional career, I have found that the way we strive to communicate scientific concepts to students through inquiry is the same way we, as educators, should learn how to teach science as inquiry. The majority of activities that have proven to be the most beneficial are the activities that first provide the foundation of a concept followed by an investigation of how the concept can be implemented. Having colleagues in schools, professional associations, and universities who offer the same guidance but differing perspectives has been key in evaluating my ability to teach science and has allowed me to explore new ways in which scientific knowledge is communicated in my classes.

WE STARTED MOVING AWAY FROM DIRECT INSTRUCTION

Liz

The state I teach in recently adopted the *Next Generation Science Standards* (*NGSS*) as our state's science standards. As my school and district prepare for the implementation of the *NGSS*, we are looking to the past for guidance. About 10 years ago, my district began a complete overhaul of our science curriculum. Not only did we switch the order in which we taught our courses, but we also began to fundamentally change how our classes were taught. We started moving away from direct instruction and toward providing students with authentic learning experiences. Because of the overwhelming success with the new curriculum sequence and the process in which we switched our curriculum, we are following a similar process as we work to implement the *NGSS* within our building and district.

District-Coherent Professional Learning

As soon as it became apparent that we would be adopting the *NGSS* as our new standards, we set to work preparing ourselves, along with the teachers in the district, for the switch to the *NGSS*. I teach and lead at a high school that is part of a two-high-school district. When we look to implement any type of change, we are required to move forward as one district, not as two individual schools. This meant that my counterpart at the other high school and I needed to be in nearly constant communication. Not only did we need to make sure that we each understood the intricacies of what we were doing, but we also needed to make sure that we shared the same information with our teachers at the same time. A lot of our early discussions were centered on when to share information, how much information to share, and who would share that information. We also discussed when we would let teachers make decisions and when we would let them provide their input, knowing full well that we wouldn't be able to reach a consensus and that we, the department chairs, would need to make some of the final decisions.

We spent a considerable amount of time providing teachers with information about the *NGSS*. We took time to share the *NGSS* and understand how the format for the standards was different from the format for the standards with which we were familiar. We focused on the concept of three-dimensional learning and how this drove the performance expectations. Teachers were able to see the science and engineering practices as a way to engage students in the disciplinary core ideas. We continued to work with the crosscutting concepts, trying to understand how they worked with the disciplinary core ideas to explain phenomena and solve problems, as this was a more difficult connection for us as a group. Much of the initial information that was shared was heavily borrowed from Achieve Inc. and the National Science Teachers Association (NSTA). The information from these organizations was thorough yet concise and provided teachers with the opportunity to initially engage as deeply as they wanted while knowing that we as a department would continue moving forward in our understanding of the *NGSS* in preparation for full implementation of the *NGSS*.

Considering the Community

After exchanging initial information about the *NGSS* with teachers, we began talking with various stakeholders within our school community. We gave tailored talks to our parent groups, elementary and middle school superintendents, the other school leaders within our building, and—most importantly—our board of education. Although we wanted to share our enthusiasm for the *NGSS*, we also wanted to prepare everyone for the changes that we would soon be experiencing. Providing all stakeholders with a similar set of background information on the *NGSS* allowed us to focus later conversations with each group of people as we made necessary decisions about teaching and learning in which they needed to be involved.

Becoming More Familiar With the NGSS

Although we, as department chairs, were sharing information with all of our stakeholders, we also began to branch out in how we accommodated teachers and their professional learning. We scheduled time during our weekly department meetings to have teachers work with the *NGSS* and not just read about them. We wanted teachers to interact with the documents so that it would support their understanding of them. In a series of meetings, we had teachers literally cut up and arrange the performance expectations into our existing course structure. We also partnered with a local university to have a few of their *NGSS* experts present to our staff. Teachers participated in authentic, three-dimensional learning experiences, which challenged them to think about their instruction differently. During this time, we were also willing to send teachers out to gain more information about the *NGSS* from local workshops. Teachers were well aware of their own understanding levels and were able to select professional development opportunities that were tailored to their needs.

As teachers became more familiar with the *NGSS*, we upped the ante and continued to push them to think and rethink their courses. This was done through careful questioning and continued professional development. After significant planning time during the preceding school year and summer, one of our content teams decided that it was ready to adopt a modified *NGSS* sequence for the current school year, and we supported this team. This benefited us all in a few different ways. Instead of all of the science courses changing at once, it allowed a small group of teachers

to truly wrestle with the content, curriculum, and teaching style that would be necessary to address the *NGSS*. This process also empowered a group of educators who were willing to share their successes and challenges with others in an open manner. Finally, it allowed us to continue the conversation about the *NGSS* in a much broader sense, using concrete evidence from this pilot course.

We have not yet fully implemented the *NGSS* as a state or school. As we prepare for our full implementation, we are beginning to focus on what the *NGSS* look like in our school as well as our district in 1, 5, and 10 years and even further out. We want our courses to change to accommodate the three-dimensional learning inherent in the *NGSS*, and we want our courses to be sustainable if and when we bring different teachers onto our content teams. We want teachers to understand the benefits that will come from making these changes and to be excited by the learning that takes place in their classrooms.

THEY ARE TEACHING ME

Mike

As I wrote before, the department is at the heart of our professional learning, and one of the greatest strengths we have is our collegiality. I have been in the department now for 15 years, and I can talk to anyone about our

work because we're speaking the same language. This doesn't happen by accident, and we are constantly looking to improve how we work. For this to happen, however, both teachers and students must be able to take risks without fear that mistakes might penalize them.

Supported by the Work of Others

There is always a component of professional reading disseminated by the chair to the department. It often connects the world of research in faculties of education to our world of application. It also connects us to what exemplary teachers and departments are doing elsewhere on the continent and around the world. The readings include primary research papers and pertinent articles from professional journals that apply to what we are focusing on in our teaching and in our own action research. We don't have to agree with all of it—the purpose is to generate self-reflection and then conversation.

Planning With Colleagues

Personally, I love chatting with Steve because he is brilliant at representing science in ways that apply directly to his lessons. It's a real talent. We also share and examine exemplars of student work between us because, again, we are all pulling in the same direction. Knowing we are going in the same direction allows me to take the risk—the opportunity—with my students to become a facilitator in the role of a senior researcher. The whole point of teaching a more accurate representation of science is for them to understand what the process is. I don't know as much as some of these kids do about their problem because I'm not doing the experiment. I'm not expected to know absolutely everything about their experiment. They're the ones who are learning

about the little details and the history during their research. I don't need to do the research for them, although I always make sure that they are safe and considering safety in their designs. I just need to teach them how to do research and how to go about the practices of science. They are teaching me.

Here's an example of how a portion of the conversation might go. This question might be asked: "Why is having only two conditions, hot and cold, or 10°C and 30°C, ineffective when you are studying the effect of temperature on the breathing rate of a fish? Why is having only two temperatures not enough?" They might respond with something like, "two conditions will give you two points on a graph, and you won't know if it's a curve or a line that's being demonstrated and the work is flawed in the sense that the error hasn't furthered our understanding of the question." They might go on to say that "getting five points on the graph, five temperature situations, will give them a shape or a curve and give them an idea of the pattern. Twenty-five would be better, but it's time and money that limits it." Then later, when I talk to them about trials, they'll say, "We need enough trials so that we trust each point. We trust that each one is a good point on that graph." That's neat for me to see them really understanding the need to collect sufficient, relevant data. Thinking about the problem and talking about their thinking is really what's going on here … meta-cognition. I wouldn't have been able to teach that concept 10 years ago. These interview sessions become assessment conversations on my part and self- and peer-reflection moments for the students as they move the work forward. Of course, to be able to carry out this kind of work means that any teacher must have the fundamentals of classroom management down. But the benefits ... this is a fertile and encouraging classroom environment in which to grow learning, where respect and feedback are a two-way street and everyone is held accountable to a high standard.

Instructional Rounds and Common Assessments

How does my classroom work fit into the teaching and learning of science that the department promotes? One way that developed from the assessment and evaluation initiative I talked about in Chapter 5 is a strategy called "instructional rounds," which enables teachers to experiment with new assessment and evaluation theory in their classrooms while their peers make observations about student interactions. We have found these instructional rounds and the subsequent peer discussions so valuable that we have incorporated them into our own departmental professional learning practices.

Another way our department worked together was to make the grade 9 exam a culminating performance in which the students carry out a formal research project, exhibit the product, and finally demonstrate their proficiency or understanding in an interview or defense with me and another teacher. I have 13 specific things that I want them to talk about, and I direct the conversation that way. This oral defense ends up being a conversation that is more than just me asking a question, listening to a response, and then writing down a mark. We'll ask a question and they'll start talking. Then we are interjecting with a supplementary question or comment. The next thing you know, there's a whole lot of learning that has gone on, even while I have been assessing their understanding of the original question. I have often said to my chair and colleagues that this is powerful because the learning doesn't stop just because it's an exam and the students are getting feedback within the structure of the exam. When does that ever happen with traditional departmental exams? Using this strategy, the teacher takes the role of the lead learner in a conversation about science. In the end, my understanding of how students learn has been magnified by the kind of professional development I've been describing.

I SPENT A LOT OF TIME IN THE LITERATURE

Steve

When the department was first experimenting with and developing strategies for the teaching of a reformed vision of science and then looking at the products of that work, I spent a lot of time in the reform literature. I worked through multiple textbooks looking for those "cookbook" experiments that were not only a good fit with our reformed curriculum but could also be adapted into formative opportunities or full-blown scientific inquiries for the students. Our chair also provided a constant stream of professional reading for us about research into reforms in science teaching and learning and journal articles about teaching or assessment strategies that other science teachers were using in their practices. We could read and reflect on these and look for material that could translate to our practices or be modified to allow that to happen. I also got a lot of ideas for culminating performances from those readings.

Grounding Work With Students

One must understand that this foundational work was helped by the collegiality and openness of discussion within our department. Developing ideas is so much easier if it's more than one person like we've done with our department. At this stage in my career, I am very good at coming up with and developing activities that promote the practices of science for students. My students need to be able to make sense of both science content and practice, and I'm the facilitator who ties the two together.

The reforms to assessment have really complemented our earlier work with the practices of science. There has been a significant impact on both myself and the students in learning to state learning goals and then going the extra mile to make them student friendly and explicit. I'm basically saying, "Here's where we're going and this is how we're going to get there." It's a chance for students and the teacher to communicate together about what the learning will entail, and questions can straighten out any misunderstandings or misconceptions. Giving meaning and reason for the learning is motivational. Maybe, for example, you're explaining to them that today's learning goal has direct implications for future career choices. We pay a lot of attention to stating learning goals up front, decoding them for the students, and helping them see what scientific concepts they should be able to understand at the end of the day. It's bigger than that, though, because the goals build to form a deeper understanding for a unit and then a broad awareness and understanding throughout the course. It has to be a continuous process, and it makes or breaks kids' learning. That's why I like to concentrate on the practices of science—the overall body of created science knowledge is too massive to memorize anymore. Sure, there are essential concepts one must master in a unit and a course because they are foundational blocks on which more learning can be built, but students should also be very aware of and comfortable working with the research practices that real-world scientists, engineers, and researchers use.

WE SEE OPPORTUNITIES TO GROW PROFESSIONALLY

Julie

Educational change can be initiated from the top down, from the bottom up, or through a mixed approach. Top-down change initiatives have the advantage that formal leaders have the time to investigate and strategically prepare and implement a change, but the drawback is that teachers can feel alienated from the change attempt (Berman and McLaughlin 1978). On the other hand, bottom-up change engages teachers immediately, but the drawback here is that teachers often lack the time, resources, and sophisticated epistemological understanding of the reform needed to fully prepare and implement the change (Berman and McLaughlin 1978). Although both of these approaches have their benefits and limitations, Darling-Hammond (2001) suggests allowing them to work in tandem: Foster bottom-up change with top-down support, structure, and sustenance.

Piquing Interest of Teachers

One approach leaders can take to merge "top-down-guided, bottom-up change" mirrors a common method used to hook students: strategically sharing information. This starting point for piquing curiosity is seen in the 5E approach to lesson planning developed by BSCS (Biological Sciences Curriculum Study; see Bybee 2015). Teachers strategically share information to Engage students, and then they provide time for students to Explore the information. A similar pattern can be seen in Havelock and Zlotolow's (1995) CREATER change model, in which leaders carefully consider how to strategically share information during the Care stage and then provide time for participants to explore ideas during the Examine stage.

I use the Care stage to investigate internal data (such as enrollment, morale, and student needs) and external information (such as articles, conference materials, and projects in other schools). This stage usually requires me to close my door and set aside a decent chunk of time to seriously examine our department, our students, and the trends in education. My goal is to emerge from this stage with nuggets to share with my colleagues that might serve as seeds that eventually grow into us questioning the status quo. Two examples adapted from other schools I've worked with illustrate how leaders plan to involve teachers in the change process through professional development avenues:

- Care stage science lab notebook example: A teacher attends a conference and learns about lab notebooks as a way to promote student ownership of knowledge. Both the teacher and the department chair love the idea! The department chair pulls some articles and talks with department chairs at other schools who have used lab notebooks.

- Care stage grade distribution example: The department chair gathers data that indicate that 35% of their freshmen earn Ds or Fs, whereas that percentage is closer to 15% for the sophomore and junior classes. The group of freshman science teachers at this particular school has been through a lot of changes over the years, and they are wary of additional changes to their approach to teaching. The department chair understands this but feels that if the teachers knew about these data, they'd be motivated to investigate the cause of this grade disparity.

In these examples of department chairs examining internal data and external information, it's clear that we see opportunities to grow professionally with the teachers in our department. The question is "How do we move to the next stage?" And is it possible to promote bottom-up change with top-down nurturing and support?

Supporting Teachers to Dig Deeper

In the CREATER change model, change agents move from the Care stage to the Relate stage to the Examine stage. Let's assume that the department chairs in these examples have already established good personal and professional relationships with their teachers, so they can move to the Examine stage.

- Examine stage science lab notebook example: The department chair asks the teacher who attended the conference to share what she learned at a department meeting. A few weeks later, the department chair asks teachers to read an article on student ownership of their knowledge. This is then discussed at the next meeting. During this discussion, the teacher who attended the conference asks if anyone would like to join her in piloting the use of lab notebooks. The department chair says that she will arrange a day for teachers to visit other schools that use lab notebooks and to plan their implementation in a pilot run.

- Examine stage grade distribution example: The department chair distributes an article on how students' experiences in the sciences affect their views of themselves as learners. He then arranges mixed grade level groups of teachers to discuss this article at their department meeting, followed by a whole-group share-out. A few weeks later, he shares the grade distribution information with his freshman-level teachers. He gives time for them to reflect, then joins them as they process what might be causing this difference. His goal is to allow them to work through feelings of defensiveness and guide them to constructive brainstorming. As they explore ideas, he provides support in the form of time to work together, to visit other classrooms, and to attend conferences. He continually encourages this group and publicly recognizes their hard work and innovation by asking them to share their experiences with others in the department.

- What I love about this model of change is that although formal leaders might have an idea of where they'd like processes to head, it is the teachers, the classroom experts, who contemplate the information and begin to articulate why and how they can work to

improve teaching and learning in their classrooms.

During the Examine stage, because we are talking about change and challenging the status quo, there is a good chance that there will be resistance. If that is the case and teachers truly had time to contemplate the implications of the shared information and they still felt that there wouldn't be enough benefit for the cost, then the experts in your department have provided you with valuable feedback—and yes, the idea is shelved, at least temporarily. However, if teachers didn't have enough time or energy to focus on the new idea, situations could be reconstructed to allow for additional time and thought on the information, and feedback should be gathered to determine if, or how, to revisit the issue.

On the other hand, if even one teacher considers a change worth trying, then this is the opportunity for formal leaders to create the professional learning environment for that teacher to experiment and learn and then share their experiences with others. From there, more teachers might give the change a try themselves, and the change can begin to take hold.

Commentary on Activities That Promote Professional Learning

Each vignette makes it clear that teachers in departments do not learn as isolated individuals. Underpinning the stories that each of our colleagues has told are strong personal and professional relationships. Working from those relationships allows teachers to engage with their colleagues in the full range of professional learning activities described in the framework developed by Timperley et al. (2007). Equally importantly, this engagement is centered on the classroom, allowing teachers to make sense of reforms in their own classrooms. There are differences, however, in how each of our colleagues represents the activities that promote professional learning. As a beginning teacher, Shawn is simultaneously working on developing relationships with his colleagues while learning from, and with, them. Mike and Steve both value having worked with their colleagues for 15 years but are always looking for strategies that hone their teaching and learning. Liz and Julie recognize the existence and value of relationships, which allows them to structure professional learning activities in ways best suited to their contexts. The net result of the vignettes is to underscore the importance of collaboration, community, and information in developing professional learning activities.

Collaboration

Shawn began his teaching career in a way that would be familiar to many of us—fulfilling temporary contracts covering for other teachers. And yet he was already questioning the didactic teaching strategies of his own science education. More than questioning, he was actively challenging them and working to replace old theories with new ones. Although his situation was not ideal in terms of developing long-term relationships, he seized every opportunity "to learn from other science teachers." Initially, this learning was related directly to his immediate needs in the classroom, supplying instructional materials and advice on how students learn. From this foundation, the activities became more focused, such as providing feedback on classroom observations (with Shawn as both the observed and the observer), discussing how to incorporate new knowledge and skills into a developing teaching repertoire, and understanding the theory behind a teaching activity or strategy. Collaboration demands that these discussions not be just one-way flows of information; there is always a recognition that "we may not have agreed on everything" but that any decision had to be based on self-reflection and subject to revision. For Shawn, collaboration has now extended into working with external organizations and universities, a hallmark of the other vignettes in this chapter.

Collaboration in Liz's department built on earlier successful curriculum reforms and followed a particular structure. Although the change to the *NGSS* was mandated, the professional learning activities were sequenced to provide teachers with opportunities to progressively understand the reform. Initially, this meant understanding the basic structure of the reform and its major components: "We took time to share the *NGSS* documentation … and encourage teachers to interact with the documents [and] understand the material." This work was enhanced by working with external expertise. Importantly, teachers collaborated in working with the reforms and were given opportunities "to select professional development opportunities that were tailored to their needs." This statement raises an important point: Teachers as professionals need to be trusted to identify their professional learning needs within the work of the department and be given the opportunity to address those needs. Teachers in Liz's department were able to pursue their individual professional learning needs within a structure that set aside realistic time for collaborative planning and implementation. As a result, one group of teachers was "ready to adopt a modified *NGSS* sequence for the current school year, and we supported [them]." By supporting and continuing to working with these teachers as they wrestled with implementing the *NGSS* in their classrooms, the department was "empowered as a group of educators who were willing to share their successes and challenges with others in an open manner." Such collaboration also allowed them to develop their conversations "in a much broader sense, using concrete evidence from this pilot course." In an environment where the implementation of reforms is often meant to be instantaneous, Liz's department highlights that successful implementation requires collaboration and time.

Although Mike is a highly experienced teacher, he is also deeply committed to collaborating with his colleagues to improve the teaching and learning that is offered both in his classroom and across the department. Collaboration for Mike takes many forms but is underpinned by an important contextual factor: Teachers and students "must be able to take risks without fear that mistakes might penalize them." This factor allows for different views to be expressed and debated across a range of activities, from conversations to sharing exemplars to classroom observations and assisting with the assessment of culminating activities. Professional reading is encouraged, but "we don't have to agree with all of it. The purpose is to generate self-reflection and then conversation." Safe in the direction that the department has adopted allows Mike "to take the risk—the opportunity—with my students to become a facilitator in the role of a senior researcher." In turn, taking this risk opens up opportunities for further collaborations, with his colleagues coming into his classroom to make observations that then drive peer discussions. Active collaboration allows an experienced teacher to learn and teach in a way that more accurately represents science in the classroom: "meta-cognition. I wouldn't have been able to teach that concept 10 years ago."

Steve also values collaboration with his colleagues and contributes to this collaboration by an active engagement with the reform literature and experimentation with the knowledge that he has gleaned from those sources: "I worked through multiple textbooks looking for those 'cookbook' experiments that were not only a good fit with our reformed curriculum but could also be adapted into formative opportunities or full-blown scientific inquiries for the students." This individual work was supplemented by departmental readings provided by the chair: "We could read and reflect on these and look for stuff that could translate to our practices or be modified to allow that to happen." As a result of this work, Steve is able to develop materials that help his students "make sense of both science content and practice, and I'm the facilitator who ties the two together." Mike also recognizes Steve's abilities: "Personally, I love chatting with Steve because he is brilliant at representing science in ways that apply directly to his lessons."

Questioning current teaching and learning practices in areas of strategic interest is a key goal of collaboration in Julie's department. As simply asking questions is unlikely to promote collaboration, teachers also need access to information drawn from a range of sources and the "time … to explore ideas." With this structure of collaboration, "it is the teachers, the classroom experts, who contemplate the information and begin to articulate why and how they can work to improve teaching and learning in their classrooms." Based on these conversations at this stage, teachers can be provided with a range of professional learning activities that will help them address their questions—from professional reading to classroom observations and the provision of instructional materials. An important point that Julie raises in the vignette is that providing a structure in which collaboration can occur is not enough. Teacher leaders must also attend to the emotional needs of teachers. Change is never easy, especially when we are asked to change practices and beliefs that can be deeply rooted in our work. One chair that Julie worked with guided his teachers through their "feelings of defensiveness" to the point where they could engage in "constructive brainstorming." He also encouraged the teachers and recognized the expertise that they had developed through their "hard work and innovation by asking them to share their experiences with others in the department." In descriptions of the department's structures for collaboration and addressing the emotional needs of teachers, each vignette highlights how departments can function as communities that promote professional learning.

Community

First, some theory, as *community* is one of those words in education jargon that has as many definitions as there are authors. For our purposes here, we are using the definition that underpinned our first book, *Reimagining the Science Department* (NSTA Press, 2015). On pages 12 and 13, we described a community as "a group of teachers who share a common sense of identity, a common sense of what it means to be a science teacher, and a relatively common set of instructional strategies." As science teachers, our education (and success) in the sciences gives us a sense of purpose as to what is important in our subject, what is important in how that content should be taught, and why it is important that it be taught. It is the science department, as a community, that determines what "good" science teaching looks like. If that departmental vision aligns with reform visions such as the *Framework* and the *NGSS*, then good. If it doesn't align, then we have some work to do—forever mindful that no department is perfect.

Shawn's vignette is interesting in that he found it difficult to "build community" due to continual moves. Despite that claim, he was actually exhibiting behaviors that indicate that he belonged to a wider community of science teachers. For example, he came to realize that he could learn from a variety of teachers, not just those who he agreed with: "Given the myriad of different teaching styles and the willingness of colleagues to share their expertise, I was able to pull what I found most useful from each style and incorporate these aspects into my own pedagogy." Such an eclectic mix worked for Shawn, as he was guided by an overarching philosophy of what he believed science teaching looked like—a philosophy that was based on his own reflection and preservice education in science education and refined by further work with courses of study. Shawn also makes the important point that the science education community is wider than the teachers he works with—it includes his colleagues involved with the courses and programs that he has been actively involved in. We say *actively* involved in, as Shawn used this wider community as a way of constantly refining his teaching: "The perspectives of colleagues and those of my professors have challenged some of my teaching strategies and positively reinforced others."

Liz also described how the science education community is wider than just the teachers in her school. At first glance, it is "within our building and district," but on closer inspection it is far wider and includes university colleagues, teacher professional associations such as NSTA, and beyond.

Liz's situation is unique in that the two high schools are required to work together: "We … move forward as one district, not as two individual schools." This raises the question of coordinating the work of the community to develop a common sense of identity, meaning, and practice, and at the heart of this is communication. Timely and accurate communication is essential if all of the members of the community are to feel that their participation is valued. Without meaningful communication, communities cannot develop, and we risk remaining in our own classrooms with our own practices. Liz also takes communication further, communicating the work of the science teachers to a wider community of "parent groups, elementary and middle school superintendents, the other school leaders within our building, and—most importantly—our board of education." Such a strategy is useful, as we discussed in Chapter 4; support for reform is built over time, built on trusting relationships, and built deliberately with the support of administrators. Finally, Liz raises three important points about the work of building community. First, it should not be seen as more work—it needs to be incorporated into the existing work of teachers and their departments: "Our weekly department meetings … have teachers work with the *NGSS*." Second, communities are not fixed; teachers come and go, and there is always work to be done to refine teaching and learning: "We want our courses to change to accommodate the three-dimensional learning … we want our courses to be sustainable if and when we bring different teachers onto our content teams." Third, teachers need to see the benefits of being involved in the community, not just for them but also for their students: "We want teachers to understand the benefits that will come from making these changes and to be excited by the learning that takes place in their classrooms."

For Mike and Steve, the department as a community has been developing for 15 years and continues to evolve. Interestingly, their experience of the department reiterates many of the points made by Shawn and Liz, thus supporting the veracity of their observations. Their department is based on collegiality and the development of a common language and understanding as to what a more accurate representation of science looks like in the classroom. This understanding has not developed in isolation—there is interaction with research, learning from other departments, experimentation with teaching, and assessment in class that is then scrutinized, as well as involvement with initiatives at the provincial level.

At another level, Mike and Steve's vignettes both show the powerful impact that a department committed to professional learning can have on the classroom practices of individual teachers. Mike is prepared to take risks in his classroom, knowing that he is working to align his classroom with the direction that the department is traveling in. Such a stance is a strong defense against idiosyncratic teaching and thus provides a sense of continuity for students in their learning. Although he is taking responsibility for his own learning, he is also sharing his learning with the department through the instructional rounds strategy and its associated observations and peer discussions, as well as involving his colleagues in the assessment of the culminating task. Steve is adamant about the virtues of professional learning that engages the entire department: "Developing ideas is so much easier if it's more than one person … like we've done with our department." Understanding and being supportive of a reformed departmental philosophy gives a global justification for his classroom practices:

> It's bigger than that, though, because the goals build to form a deeper understanding for a unit and then a broad awareness and understanding throughout the course. It has to be a continuous process, and it makes or breaks kids' learning. That's why I like to concentrate on the practices of science—the overall body of created science knowledge is too massive to memorize anymore.

As in Liz's department, professional learning is seen as an integral part of teachers' work, not as an optional extra.

Julie's vignette addresses the need for teacher leaders to be mindful of how they conceptualize the community that they are working to implement. Communities require work to develop and maintain, and both of these tasks require credible and respected leadership. We cannot afford to follow the advice attributed to Ledru-Rollin: "There go the people. I must follow them, for I am their leader." Julie recognizes that formal leaders can investigate, plan, and implement a change but that "teachers can feel alienated from the change attempt." Conversely, waiting for change is hardly an option, as teachers often lack "the time, resources, and sophisticated epistemological understanding of the reform needed to fully prepare and implement the change." As Julie suggests, developing a community requires leadership that plants "seeds that eventually grow into us questioning the status quo." A credible leader can then work with those questions to start building a community in which teachers can "experiment and learn and then … share their experiences with others. From there, more teachers might give the change a try themselves, and the change can begin to take hold." Start small, grow from there, and be mindful that resistance is part of community building. As Julie wisely says, if your teachers

> *truly had time to contemplate the implications of the shared information and they still felt that there wouldn't be enough benefit for the cost, then the experts in your department have provided you with valuable feedback—and yes, the idea is shelved, at least temporarily. However, if teachers didn't have enough time or energy to focus on the new idea, situations could be reconstructed to allow for additional time and thought on the information, and feedback should be gathered to determine if, or how, to revisit the issue.*

The role of information is central in shaping the professional learning activities of each of our colleagues, and it is the final issue that we wish to explore in this commentary.

Information

All of our colleagues rely on information to inform the professional learning activities that they engage in or lead. The reliance on information that has been documented is interesting in that it highlights both individual motivations for seeking out professional learning activities and also how information can influence the professional learning activities that are sequenced for departments.

As a relatively inexperienced teacher, Shawn has been shaped by the information that he received in his teacher education program. Even as he suspected that the way in which he was being taught was not as effective as he might have wished, he was able to recognize the change from direct instruction to a more reformed stance toward teaching and learning: "The knowledge I gained was not simply put into practice as per teacher instructions but rather as a guided inquiry." Coming to this understanding was important for Shawn, as the application of this knowledge has guided every subsequent professional learning activity that he has engaged in. As Fullan (1992) wrote, action on knowledge is imperative, for it is through "informed experiments, pursuing promising directions, and testing out and refining new arrangements and practices that we make the most headway" (p. 63). Part of making this headway is to inquire into increasingly sophisticated aspects of Shawn's practice such as "re-evaluating the use and effectiveness of science textbooks … addressing student misconceptions in biology and chemistry, and creating student-designed inquiry-based lab instructions."

Mike and Steve are immersed in a departmental culture that values information. As such, they have ready access to professional readings, which for Mike links "the world of research in faculties of education to our world of application [and] to what exemplary teachers and departments were doing elsewhere on the continent and around the world." This is not just information for the sake of information. For Steve, working through textbooks and reform literature opens up opportunities to look "for material that could translate to our practices or be modified to allow that to happen." Research literature provided by the chair is important to Steve and Mike, who related the material to "what we are focusing on in our teaching and in our own action research." This is information that serves a strategic purpose: "to generate self-reflection and then conversation." The order here is interesting— the conversations follow the reflection and comparison with existing practice. The result is that the information can be considered in the context of linking both the departments' and individuals' professional learning. For the chair, information on reforms—and what to do with it—is always a vexed issue in departments.

The vignettes by Liz and Julie highlight two different strategies for dealing with questions of information. Both strategies work in these departments because both Liz and Julie have placed a premium on developing strong relationships with their teachers, and both have very different work situations. Both strategies, however, start in the same place. For both Liz and Julie, the crucial first stage in using information to shape professional learning activities is to understand the information. For Liz, this means that "we each [understand] the intricacies of what we [are] doing." For Julie, it means closing "my door and [setting] aside a decent chunk of time to seriously examine our department, our students, and the trends in education." From this initial understanding, we then have two very different ways of using that information.

Liz is working on introducing the *NGSS* in concert with a chair in another school and must coordinate everything with the other chair. This coordination also involves deciding "when to share information, how much information to share, and who would share that information." Not only was the dissemination of information planned, but the chairs also discussed "when we would let teachers make decisions and when we would let them provide their input, knowing full well that we wouldn't be able to reach a consensus and that we, the department chairs, would need to make some of the final decisions." Such decisions can only be made with any sort of confidence when there is a strong relationship between a chair and the department and a high level of trust in the judgment of the chair. The approach Julie takes is also predicated on relationships and trust, but of a different form. Julie knows her department and works strategically to address issues of teaching and learning. She trusts them to take the information that she shares with them so that it "might serve as seeds that eventually grow into us questioning the status quo."

Although these ways of using information are different, the professional learning activities that followed were remarkably similar. Both chairs stressed working with the information to understand and then transfer knowledge of the material to the classroom. If extra information or external perspectives on the information were needed, these were sought out. In both cases, there was an expectation that teachers would be involved in this work of translating the information into practice but also an understanding that some teachers would be more involved than others "as deeply as they wanted" (Liz). In Julie's example, "The department chair asks the teacher who attended the conference to share what she learned [and] asks if anyone would like to join her in piloting the use of lab notebooks."

An important aspect of engaging teachers is that they know supports are available to pursue the work that they are doing. In Julie's example, the chair arranged "a day for teachers to visit other schools that use lab notebooks and to plan their implementation in a pilot run." In Liz's department, "this was done through careful questioning and continued professional development."

Conclusion

The vignettes highlight the breadth of activities that teachers can engage in when they are looking to reform their practices. From in-class observations, to reading, considering, and then enacting reform, to developing close professional relationships, to participating in professional learning communities, all of our colleagues participate in a range of activities. In every vignette, the work of professional learning is not an individual undertaking. The closest we have to individualism is Steve working through literature looking for material that can work or be adapted into the departmental philosophy on teaching and learning. And even this activity is a precursor to working with other teachers on the reforms.

There is no one best professional learning strategy—teacher leaders have a responsibility to provide a range of activities suited to their particular department and context. Liz and Julie, as department chairs, were clear that the range of those activities needed to be based on information about the learning needs of their colleagues and the reforms the department was looking to implement. Information needs to be related to teachers' practices, not just confirmatory. Ideally, information should also challenge and serve as a catalyst for reflection and then action leading to reform.

Finally, working with information within departments that encourage a collegial questioning of practice and experimentation with reformed teaching and learning raises questions of the processes by which teachers learn. This is the topic of the final set of vignettes.

Summary

- No single activity will promote teacher professional learning; rather, we know that activities need to be actively embedded in the subject matter, connected to teachers' extant practices, and coherent across the scope of reform documents.

- Teachers in departments do not learn as isolated individuals; instead, they build and rely on strong personal and professional relationships with colleagues.

- Teachers as professionals need to be trusted to identify their professional learning needs within the work of the department and be given the opportunity to address those needs through engaging in collaboration with peers and being provided with the time necessary to enact and refine innovations in their classrooms.

- Providing a structure in which collaboration can occur is not enough. Teacher leaders must also attend to the emotional needs of teachers.

- A community as defined for the purposes of science departments is "a group of teachers who share a common sense of identity, a common sense of what it means to be a science teacher, and a relatively common set of instructional strategies." However, without meaningful communication, communities cannot develop, and we risk remaining in our own classrooms with our own practices.

- An important aspect of engaging teachers is that they know supports are available to pursue the work that they are doing.

Questions to Consider

1. What are the strategies you might explore to ensure that the professional activities designed to support professional learning in your department or school are actively embedded in the subject matter, connected to teachers' extant practices, and coherent across the scope of reform documents?

2. How might your department or school support strong personal and professional relationships between colleagues?

3. How has your school entrusted teachers to lead their own professional learning? What are ways your department or school might ensure that the benefits of this trust are recognizable to school and district administrators?

4. To what extent would you currently describe your department as a community that is "a group of teachers who share a common sense of identity, a common sense of what it means to be a science teacher, and a relatively common set of instructional strategies"? What strategies might be useful in strengthening your community?

5. What supports are available to teachers engaged in self-directed or community-directed professional learning, and to what extent are those engaged in professional learning aware of these supports?

The Learning Processes That Teachers Engage In

When we talk about the learning processes that teachers engage in, we are into an area potentially fraught with difficulties. From the framework developed by Timperley et al. (2007, p. 6), we know that teachers can "react in very different ways as a result of engaging in the same professional learning activities [and] that having expertise in one situation does not necessarily translate into expertise in another." Even as we acknowledge this, three learning processes are important for teachers' professional learning: "cueing and retrieving prior knowledge, becoming aware of new information and skills, and creating dissonance with a teacher's current position. These processes are not mutually exclusive: All may be present in a given professional learning opportunity" (p. 7).

For Jason and the department of which he is a member, professional learning activities have concentrated for many years on these processes:

> *For the members of our department, they help us refine so many of the great things we were experimenting with. Professional learning gave us a language and framework for the strategies that we adopted and continue to adapt over time.*

Each of our colleagues makes references to these processes in their vignettes, which is an affirmation of the framework that we are using. What is equally important are the lessons that we can draw from their experiences at different points in their careers.

AND YES, I AM GUILTY OF THAT, TOO

Shawn

Since becoming a science teacher, I have come to appreciate how diverse students are personally, socially, culturally, academically, and cognitively. Just as they are different on a personal level, their modes of thinking and how they learn are equally distinctive. Usually the focus in our education as teachers is how are we able to tap into those modes of thinking to best communicate the knowledge and experience we have. Similarly, in our professional development we often take the same seats as those who are in our classes, albeit with an older clientele, a more experienced audience, and an even more experienced educator who communicates his or her ideas and knowledge to us. I must admit that this may not always be the best way for teachers to learn, but as I share my experience in the learning processes of our professional development, I must point out that just as our students are diverse, we, too, are all just as diverse in our approaches and our receptiveness to new ideas.

Learning From Students

When I teach my classes, I have always spoken to students during the year about how to improve my delivery of material or what I can do to make my classes more engaging. Many of the ideas I learn—through workshops, courses, other colleagues, or students themselves—I have tried to incorporate in some way into my classroom. Many of my students give great feedback about how I communicate concepts and the creative ways I approach topics; they also give me new ideas of how to modify and approach different topics that may allow others to understand them more thoroughly. This has been very useful when teaching the same class in consecutive years; applying feedback from prior years to new classes and listening to current feedback after modifications builds an even stronger foundation for constructive change for future classes. In hindsight, I do have a specific philosophy to how I teach. The main challenge is looking at how I currently teach and how I could teach in the future. Many of us have a set mentality on what we think works best for student learning. And yes, I am guilty of that, too. What I continually reinforce in my own learning is the ability to build a bridge that connects what I currently believe works best with what could work better. Sometimes these can be synonymous, but as an individual with a perfectionist attitude, the dissonance between these two circumstances is the motivation I need to try new ideas to perfect my teaching style for the good of my students.

I have found the true challenge is when there is a larger disparity between ideas; for example, a traditional "sage on the stage" mentality versus a flipped classroom. For instance, when I'm teaching a concept such as organic compound naming in a traditional classroom, students would be coming to class without prior knowledge of the step-by-step procedure. In a flipped classroom, students will take responsibility and independently learn the procedure through teacher-produced instructional media; when in class, the focus can turn to developing a more thorough understanding through practice with more challenging questions or extensions of relating organic naming to real-world applications. These two strategies are completely different in their approach to teaching, and in departments where individuals are less open to change, implementing new ideas can be hard. Consistency between classes, especially in larger schools with multiple educators teaching the same course, can also provide an overwhelming barrier to change. I have found that taking small steps when working with like-minded colleagues has been valuable in implementing changes to common practice. I find that when those who are resistant to change can see the benefits to students and see that more than one teacher has implemented the change, credibility is easier to accept. This in turn allows those who are skeptical to be more receptive to learning new ideas.

Direct Observations

At one of my prior schools, the major concept they focused on in grade 9 was the scientific method. However, it was not just explaining the typical terminology of what is the problem, hypothesis, procedure, and so on. Students focused on applying the specifics of each part and designing a lab of their own. They were unrestricted in what experiments they could pursue (safety considerations, of course, were non-negotiable) and worked through their independent, dependent, and controlled variables while independently designing their procedures and evaluating the efficacy of their completed labs. Once students presented their findings in a formal in-class lab, all grade 9 students who had science that semester would have a schoolwide science fair competition that was divided by their academic levels (applied, academic, and enriched) and incorporated prizes for the most well-designed and creative labs. My thoughts on how effective this approach would be in reinforcing their knowledge of the scientific method were skeptical at best. My skepticism was predicated on the sheer volume of information these grade 9 students had to understand in such a short time on top of learning all the concepts of the grade 9 curriculum. I am more than happy to say they proved me wrong! Halfway through the year, once the fair had been completed, many students showed a comprehensive understanding of the scientific method when applying their knowledge, adapting a creative approach to their topic, and having fun at the same time!

As a result of being at that school and seeing this idea developed, I have tried to incorporate this into my current classes. So far, I have taken minor steps; I have implemented this idea on a smaller scale in my own classroom and have understood, through observation in my old school and in my current classes, the benefits that this activity holds. Hopefully, in the next few years I can present this idea to some of my more open-minded colleagues; once they see the benefit, perhaps this can be presented to other classes and eventually to an entire department. Graduating students from the classes I taught at this prior school have come back to visit; many of them still remember the science fair projects they completed when I taught them. After pursuing postsecondary education in science, they have explained that the design labs they completed had a significant impact on their understanding and love of science. Even though the project was completed in grade 9, they are still surprised at how relatable it is to their current studies and how connected the activity is to the real-world applications of scientific research. From these conversations, I have come to appreciate how beneficial this activity was for these students. I must admit that the most compelling motivation in how I learn as an educator is through direct observation of positive student outcomes; when I am thrown into a learning opportunity and I see the benefits, there is no limit to my receptiveness and eagerness to continue learning!

THERE BECAME SOME NATURAL DISSONANCE

Liz

In education, there is always something new—a new evaluation process, a new curriculum, new software, new textbooks. Sometimes these new things are rooted in solid research, and other times they are due to the words of a student, colleague, administrator, or supervisor. As a teacher and a leader, it has been my responsibility—working with our science team—to determine which of these new things are aligned with our goals and is rooted in research. We also must determine which ideas we are ready as a department to move forward with for the betterment of our teaching and our students.

The *NGSS* at the Center

We as a science department have been working with *A Framework for K–12 Science Education* (the *Framework*) and the *Next Generation Science Standards* (*NGSS*), through different public drafts, for a number of years. Initially, some of us were at the forefront of the standards, reading the *Framework*, attending workshops, networking with others, and attending conferences to learn more. Those of us who began an initial investigation into the *NGSS* did so because we were interested and curious. Our initial curiosity started because many in our state felt that the *NGSS* would become our new state standards. However, as we read and learned more, we were able to embrace what was being presented to us as the epitome of a science classroom. As it became apparent that our state would adopt the *NGSS,* my counterpart and I began a more earnest attempt to understand what the *NGSS* would look like in our classrooms. We also began planning how we were going to support teacher professional learning with resources and professional development on the *NGSS,* knowing the varied backgrounds of those within our departments.

At the district level, we strategically planned how we would spend professional development time and money. Working with the assistant principals of curriculum at each building in the district and the assistant superintendent of curriculum, we set aside grant money to pay for teachers to attend professional development. In doing this, we essentially guaranteed that any science teacher who asked about professional development opportunities could attend at least one conference or workshop focused on the *NGSS* during the school year. Teachers were then asked to share their learning with their peers during department meetings and meetings with content teams. My counterpart and I were also given one full day of professional development to plan during the school year. We partnered with a local university to bring *NGSS* training to our building. Although it was only one day, it was one day when teachers were able to participate in a workshop where, with the careful guidance of experts, teachers worked to design phenomena-driven learning experiences for students.

All of these individual professional learning experiences were reinforced during our weekly department meetings. During our regular time together, we participated in a number of different activities that encouraged teachers to work more deeply with the *NGSS* than they may have done during their normal prep periods. Sometimes we read information about the standards and discussed what that looked like in our classrooms. Sometimes we met as content teams to have professional discussions about how implementing the *NGSS* in our classrooms would be different from how we were currently teaching. Sometimes we took lessons that we thought were aligned to the *NGSS* and shared how they were—or sometimes were not—aligned. Sometimes we met to express inevitable frustration as we worked to change what was happening in our classes. Sometimes we met as cross-curricular teams to talk about the link of content within our courses and how we could share our expertise in planning and developing experiences for our students. These experiences were varied during our meetings to meet the needs of our teachers as their understanding of the *NGSS* grew, changed, and was used increasingly more in the classroom.

Our chemistry team's experience highlights how this professional learning took place in the classroom. After receiving some summer professional development training on the *NGSS,* the team reconvened to discuss how to better teach at the start of the school year, as the beginning labs often feel void of context; they are introductory labs on measuring volume and mass and include other experiences that familiarize students with the lab. The team decided to use the culminating activity—a density column—as the phenomenon to hook students and then use the previous labs on measurement to support the learning of skills for students to then build their own density column at the end of the experience as the assessment. In the first year, the team decided to jump in and try it out. Students were engaged, but few places needed improvement, so in the following years the teachers continued to modify the unit, taking into consideration initial concerns as well as new information that was gained about the *NGSS*. This lesson allowed a group of teachers to see that it was possible to engage students in a phenomenon-driven unit and, knowing that density is not a high school performance expectation, this team of teachers is working to modify other units to better reflect the content within the *NGSS*.

Natural Dissonance

As understanding of the *NGSS* grew, there became some natural dissonance with what we were doing in our classrooms and what we were coming to believe we *should* be doing in our classrooms. This dissonance was coupled with changes we were experiencing as a building in questioning if what we were doing in our instructional practices, in *all* content areas, was truly best for students. While we were working to understand the *NGSS*, there were some natural places where teachers began to question their practices. A few teachers in the department began to investigate moving toward standards-based grading, which they felt dovetailed nicely with a move to the *NGSS*. Teachers appreciated how the performance expectations in the *NGSS* share precise information about what students should know and be able to do, yet provide flexibility for students to show mastery in a number of different ways. These clearly worded performance expectations coupled with school-provided professional learning about standards-based grading provided some teachers in the department with the confidence to start making the jump. Others began to look more intently at project-based learning experiences instead of multiple-choice assessments for assessing student learning. Teachers realized that many of the experiences students were having in their classrooms were not being accurately assessed with a multiple-choice assessment. Teachers began to experiment with having projects replace standard exams as well as adding lab practicals to more typical exams to better mirror the learning that was taking place in the classroom. Although standards-based grading and project-based learning experiences are not required for successful implementation of the *NGSS*, some teachers felt that there were places where they could grow in their practices, and they felt that the *NGSS* were their springboard into a broader change in their teaching practices.

While teachers were working to understand the *NGSS* as well as the magnitude to which they wanted to change their classroom practices, I tried to support teachers in their endeavors. My end goal was to have the department ready for the state's implementation of the *NGSS*, so I worked with teachers to achieve this goal. As others came to me with spin-off ideas, I worked with them and their teams to make their goals a reality. Sometimes teachers just needed the confidence to know that they were being supported, whereas other times I was much more involved in meeting and talking teachers through their plans.

As we prepare for the final push into the initial implementation, I am proud of the work that the teachers in our department have done. They have worked together as a team to understand the *NGSS* and began designing phenomena-driven experiences for students to have in their classes. They have also begun to modify assessments to better address the skills and knowledge that students will have as a result of the *NGSS*. More importantly, teachers know that they will need to continue refining these experiences for students.

BREAKING DOWN WHAT I KNEW

Mike

As a department, we have been refining our teaching of the practices of science for many years. What we have been working on over the last few years is how our assessment strategies should more closely reflect what we have been teaching. For me, that has involved breaking down what I knew and building up a new understanding and a new range of strategies.

Breaking Down ... Building Up

For example, my students may have been working on a research report of an investigation that they have been working on. If you say it's due on Tuesday and they bring in all the pieces, I say, "OK, gang, I know it was due on Tuesday, but I'm not collecting it today. We're doing a peer edit, so get out all the success criteria and pore through those. Are you proud of it yet? What needs to be fixed up?"

Those are things that I might not have done before. Students understand that to get the best product, they have to have the opportunity to peer-assess and self-assess their work against defined success criteria. What makes a good scientific research report? So I see them reading through each other's work and going, "Wow, this is great, but did we forget to do this piece? Have we talked about experimental error?" They make their edits and share the rewrite. They'll probably share it back and forth that night on their devices. They're all checking each other's work. Mind you, that takes time to develop in students. You have to give the time for that, but the product is exponentially better.

Expanding on Assessment

The other neat piece is that when you're assessing, you're walking around, you're listening, and you're observing. Certainly you're assessing product, but you're also assessing all the conversations that they're having, and you're observing all the things that they're doing. You're armed. If you're armed with an iPad (or equivalent), you're gathering all sorts of evidence of their understanding, and not just from the final product. John and Judy might have been having a fantastic conversation about variables and about all of the learning that's been going on, right? So if you see and hear those conversations, you've got evidence of learning there. Then, if you observe them doing an absolutely amazing job of designing an experiment—in terms of keeping variables constant, for example—you again have a terrific set of assessment data. We now call it being able to make informed professional judgments with data, and it doesn't just have to be product. Not so many years ago, that evidence was only what students handed in or wrote on a test.

AGAIN, THAT'S SCIENCE

Steve

I don't agree with the concern that reformed teaching places large demands on teacher's content knowledge. Learning is ongoing—you don't (or shouldn't) stop. Sometimes my students will carry out an investigation and come up with odd data or questions and, yeah, they found out something you're not sure about or that was unexpected, but it's still in the realm of learning. It's going to lead to a great conversation and, if necessary, one or both of you can see if some research will shed some light on it. That's what real researchers are faced with. It's fun for both of us when I say, "Wow, I've never seen that before." Again, that's science. One question leads to another, we learn more about the problem, another door opens, and we move forward.

More Than Content

I think preservice teachers are full of content, but how to convey that content in a meaningful way—that's what their difficulty is, and that's why there are teaching placements. When they come into our science department, we get them into reformed teaching right away so it becomes familiar and they can concentrate on learning how to convey it to the kids. Getting in early is good for our school. It develops some beautiful preservice teachers, and they've got a leg up because they've already been exposed to reformed teaching.

I feel bad when they go on to other schools where they don't get that, and they'll go back to traditional ways of teaching science and get entrenched with that. I hope when they're done with our placement they'll go on, and remember and risk, incorporating some of what they've learned in another placement or in their first contract.

HOW CAN WE INVESTIGATE CHANGE?

Julie

Sometimes you hear about the caricature of a curmudgeonly teacher who spouts phrases like "my kids can't do that" or "that won't work with my kids." In the reality I've experienced, including the three schools I've worked in plus the multiple schools I've consulted with, I rarely hear anything like this sad stereotype. What I hear sometimes, though, is teachers' self-doubt or skepticism about the efficacy of touted reform proposals. What's reassuring is that both of these expressions of hesitance are not based on teachers' beliefs in their kids, and they're not based on teacher reluctance to work hard to make their students' lives better. When I hear teacher resistance to a new idea, it seems to mostly stem from the fact that teaching is a difficult and nuanced act, and there needs to be a good reason, and a good chance of success, to change.

Understanding Change in a System

Change is difficult in most professions, and it's the same for education. Teachers and administrators work within systems that need to be stable: The buses need to be on time, the bells need to ring as scheduled, lunch needs to be ready when the students arrive, teachers need to have their supplies, and students need to know what is expected of them. The list of items and activities that need to be stable is huge. When stability is jostled, even with something as mundane as a fire drill, it can be unsettling to the members of the organization, even when everything works out well in the end. Therefore, contemplating a change can raise educators' caution flags. However, as educators know, we need to constantly improve and constantly work to find ways to make students' lives better, so the question is "How can we investigate change while respecting our system's need for stability and consistency?"

One thing educational leaders can do to emphasize stability while introducing possible change is to create a regular program of professional development in the form of professional learning communities (PLCs). This isn't always an option depending on the structure of the school and funding, but starting change from the foundation of a PLC structure provides a forum through which teachers can explore ideas presented by the administration in a strategic and consistent format or presented by teachers as they reflect on their craft. PLCs provide space, and especially time, to consider new information, develop professional identities as continuous learners, and explore areas of change safely.

The goal of a PLC is to prompt and nurture teacher learning. This would include a mix of guiding questions, related readings or data presentations, and feedback from teachers on the topics explored as well as on their day-to-day experiences. The latter part of this PLC mix is designed to enhance teachers' feelings of trust and respect—the key is, though, that hearing teacher feedback must also be coupled with a positive response from the administration when possible. For example, if teachers feel that the shoe cubbies are not large enough in the rear of the second-grade classrooms, as it creates a chaotic feel in the back of the classroom, ask a handy parent to see what he or she can do to improve the situation. If parents are surprising teachers by showing up to chat without an appointment, institute a policy and use front staff to enforce it. Some of this feedback on day-to-day issues can be addressed fairly easily, whereas some cannot—be creative and address what is possible. Although this probably will not speak to educational reform per se, it cultivates trust in leadership, and that trust is a bedrock of stability on which teachers can lean when changes are occurring.

Trust, Then Reform

Once the bedrock of trust is in place, PLCs can be used to build teachers' understanding of reform topics incrementally. Sharing strategically chosen readings and data at PLCs can be coupled with guiding questions to prompt discussion. During discussions, teachers can express concerns, explore alternatives, and ask questions. Some of these concerns and questions can then be used as guides for further professional development, such as conference attendance, visiting other schools, additional readings, or designing in-depth data collection and analysis.

All of this takes time, strategic planning, and a Zen approach because rarely are new ideas embraced immediately. Luckily, a lack of immediate embrace does not necessarily predict failure. Resistance or skepticism is a fantastic opportunity for teachers to seriously consider the downsides of a possible change, either in general or specifically for their school. This allows for problem solving before problems actually materialize, and it allows for refinement prior to the change attempt. It also allows informal teacher leaders to emerge who can further investigate or pilot ideas and then report back to the group. From this point on, change is a teacher-led investigation, guided and supported by the administration, which builds deeper teacher understanding of reform topics over time.

Changing someone's mindset takes time, and with good reason. The effort involved in educational change can be large, and frequently so is the risk: Changes that occur too hastily or without stakeholders' input can result in spectacular failures and contempt. The building of teachers' deep understanding of reforms can take many paths, and one path that can be explored when time permits follows a sequence in which teachers trust the stability of their system, examine and explore new ideas over time as presented by the administration or colleagues, expand their circle of knowledge through additional professional development, try out ideas and take risks, and share their experiences with their colleagues. This does not guarantee buy-in or successful change, but it does provide time for all parties to seriously consider information and explore changes safely. It also provides a forum not only for continued professional growth but also for a space for leaders to hear angles on reforms that they may not have considered yet, which can prove to be useful in determining future professional development and for determining whether there is a path forward and what that path might entail.

Commentary on the Learning Processes That Teachers Engage In

In the previous three chapters, we have considered the context, content, and professional learning through the experiences of five science teachers. We have seen the changing perspectives to professional learning across teachers' careers and the impact of leadership in shaping those perspectives. Working from the framework developed by Timperley et al. (2007), we have come to see what is important to individual teachers in understanding their own professional learning needs. In many ways, this chapter draws the previous three chapters together by focusing our attention on teachers' learning and the motivation and supports needed to sustain the processes that they engage in. In particular, our colleagues have highlighted that the success of students is their core motivation, that reforms need to be addressed in a deliberate manner, and that learning processes need to be supported both cognitively and emotionally.

Motivation

All of our colleagues were explicit in placing the success of their students at the core of their work. There may be teachers who think "my kids can't do that" or "that won't work with my kids," but we believe that those teachers are the minority. The majority of teachers are committed to their students. This moral concern is a powerful motivation for change and is also key to sustaining the improvements to teaching and learning, especially when the work of reform is difficult. For Shawn, constantly seeking feedback from his students on teaching and learning has made him "appreciate how diverse students are personally, socially, culturally, academically, and cognitively." This realization has challenged him to consider "how I *currently* teach and how I *could* teach in the future." Recognizing such a dissonance is not easy—as teachers, we often "have a set mentality on what we think works best for student learning." We are often caught in a dilemma between recognizing the need for change and seeing the safety to be found in the status quo.

For Mike, professional learning means "breaking down what I knew and building up a new understanding and a new range of strategies" within his department. His colleague Steve expressed a similar opinion: "One question leads to another, we learn more about the problem, another door opens, and we move forward." Julie continued this line of thinking, pointing out, "How can we investigate change while respecting our system's need for stability and consistency?" Although stability and consistency have their value and can be reassuring in the face of seemingly constant calls for reform, a genuine concern for our students ("for the good of my students") will motivate us to connect "what I currently believe works best with what could work better." Shawn emphasized the connection between professional learning and a concern for his students: "The most compelling motivation in how I learn as an educator is through direct observation of positive student outcomes."

For Liz and her teachers, the spark of dissonance was in their response to the state decision to implement the *NGSS*. Having worked through previous topic-based reforms, understanding the *NGSS* provided a vision of what the teachers considered to be "the epitome of a science classroom." This vision aligned with growing questions as to "what we were doing in our classrooms and what we were coming to believe we *should* be doing in our classrooms." Motivating this questioning was a concern for student success—"if what we were doing in our instructional practices, in *all* content areas, was truly best for students." Mike recognized that changes in his own practice, and the benefits for his students, took time: "Those are things that I might not have done before, [but] to get the best product … you have to give the time … but the product is exponentially better." One reason Julie has been a successful chair is that she recognizes the tensions that teachers face when confronting calls for reform. She has heard the stereotypes of teacher resistance, as we all have, but she also understands that as educators "we need to constantly improve and constantly work to find ways to make students' lives better." The important argument that Julie makes in her vignette is that teachers' concerns for their students' success are often tempered by a "self-doubt or skepticism about the efficacy of touted reform proposals." Although teachers are highly motivated to provide the best for their students, they also understand (better than anyone else) that "teaching is a difficult and nuanced act, and there needs to be a good reason, and a good chance of success, to change." This is the second point that we draw from the vignettes.

Being Deliberate

Each vignette reinforces the notion that teachers are open to reform but need to see that the reforms are credible and will promote teaching and learning. From Shawn to Julie, the message is consistent—a healthy skepticism can guide professional learning by giving teachers permission to question and experiment with the reform. These processes are not linear, they tend not to happen in a hurry, and they also require an honesty to admit that our current practices may not be meeting the real needs of our students or subject. As the economist John Maynard Keynes is attributed with saying: "When the facts change, I change my mind. What do you do, sir?"

For Shawn, the reforms that present the greatest challenge are those that have the largest "disparity between ideas." Skepticism can underpin these perceptions, and this skepticism must be identified and addressed: "My skepticism was predicated on the sheer volume of information these grade 9 students had to understand in such a short time. ... I am more than happy to say they proved me wrong!" To deliberately work through reforms and our skepticism is not a short-term proposition. For Shawn, it means a minimum of three years of work, from "applying feedback from prior years to new classes" to "listening to current feedback after modifications" to building "constructive change for future classes." The context is also significant to Shawn; a shared commitment to reform is important, especially in "larger schools with multiple educators teaching the same course, [which] can also provide an overwhelming barrier to change." In such cases, being deliberate involves taking "small steps when working with like-minded colleagues [when] implementing changes to common practice."

Steve takes this argument a step further to include preservice teachers on placement in his department. For Steve, subject knowledge is not an issue: "I think preservice teachers are full of content, but how to convey that content in a meaningful way ... that's what their difficulty is. ... I feel bad when they go on to other schools [and go] back to traditional ways of teaching science." For Steve, educating the next generation of science teachers means supporting them as they make the change from being a student to becoming a reform-minded teacher. Without that support, he warns, they will teach as they were taught. Liz and her department made conscious, research-based decisions as to what professional learning should be focused on. Such decisions are not to be rushed; they must represent the "epitome of a science classroom" and should lead to the "betterment of our teaching and students." A key advantage of focusing on one decision is that it allows teachers to consolidate their thoughts and practices in that area before moving on to related areas that identify themselves through the teachers' work: "There were places where they could grow in their practices, and they felt that the *NGSS* were their springboard into a broader change in their teaching practices."

Liz also warns that being deliberate does not guarantee that professional learning is without risk. Being deliberate is useful in that it provides a goal to work toward, and this can sustain teachers when things are not going as planned: "Sometimes we met to express inevitable frustration as we worked to change what was happening in our classes."

Julie's vignette reflects the value of deliberation in undertaking reform. As a highly experienced chair, Julie recognizes that providing time to deliberate gives teachers opportunities to question and develop a deeper understanding of what is required of them: "Resistance or skepticism is a fantastic opportunity for teachers to seriously consider the downsides of a possible change. … This allows for problem solving before problems actually materialize, and it allows for refinement prior to the change attempt."

More prosaically, Julie points out that "changes that occur too hastily or without stakeholders' input can result in spectacular failures and contempt." If we wish to avoid spectacular failure or contempt, then we need to ensure that learning processes are supported cognitively and emotionally. This is our third point.

Supporting Learning Processes

People learn in different ways, but learning takes time, is always a risk, and must be seen as worthwhile. In their seminal 1982 paper, Posner et al. wrote that learning comes with several conditions attached. To learn, there must be dissatisfaction with the current situation, what is being proposed must be intelligible, and the new ideas must be perceived as initially plausible. For science departments, these conditions must be dealt within the community of the department. To expect individual teachers to change is unrealistic: The life of the "lone inquirer is difficult" (Dana and Yendol-Silva 2003, p. 7). Without ongoing support, it is difficult for individual teachers to "focus on the harder things that teachers must do—such as developing habits of mind" (Shinohara quoted in Mundry 2005, p. 13). Without support, as Steve argued in relation to preservice teachers, it is relatively easy to "go back to traditional ways of teaching science and get entrenched with that."

Julie's explicit description of departments as PLCs provides a template for visualizing the supports that learning processes require—both cognitive and emotional. Although your context may be different, there are important lessons to learn from Julie's vignette, lessons that are reiterated by each of our other colleagues. The first is that the department provides a "forum through which teachers can explore ideas" that are generated by administrators, curriculum and reform documents, and teachers themselves. We are not talking short term here—three to five years will be the minimum amount of time to address reforms in a "strategic and consistent" manner. Liz's department took a number of years to work through Physics First before adopting similar strategies with the implementation of the *NGSS*. Shawn is working with ideas and with colleagues from a previous school and will bring that work to his current colleagues, "hopefully, in the next few years." The structure in each case is deceptively simple: It provides "space, and especially time, to consider new information, develop professional identities as continuous learners, and explore areas of change safely."

Second, structures that support learning need to be flexible, as teachers' understanding of reforms can, in Julie's words, "take many paths." This means that departments need to be well connected to a range of professional learning providers and opportunities, such as professional associations and their resources, conferences, and the expertise that exists in neighboring schools, local universities, and board or district initiatives.

Finally, we must not overlook that in undertaking reforms to teaching and learning, we are asking teachers to take risks. To challenge what we know and what we believe has been successful in the past with new knowledge and practices is a daunting practice. Of course, the trade-off can be huge, as Mike stated: "We now call it being able to make informed professional judgments with data, and it doesn't just have to be product. Not so many years ago, that evidence was only what students handed in or wrote on a test." Regardless of the outcome, the reform of teaching and learning is emotionally draining. All of our colleagues have spoken of teachers working together to gather and consider information, working through new teaching and learning strategies in their classrooms, questioning the value and credibility of the reforms, and reporting back to their colleagues what they had found. In all of these learning processes, structures had been built that engendered a high level of trust, as we discussed in Chapter 4. Taking risks is only tolerable when we are also prepared to accept frustrations, mistakes, and disappointments. Working deliberately and taking Shawn's "small steps" may help ameliorate the risks, but a crucial feature in the work of our colleagues is that they felt that there was always someone to work through issues with. As Liz stated, "Sometimes teachers just needed the confidence to know that they were being supported."

Conclusion

In the introduction to this chapter, we wrote that understanding teachers' learning processes can be an area of potential difficulty. Each of our colleagues has mentioned or implied the three processes discussed by Timperley et al. (2007, p. 7): "cueing and retrieving prior knowledge, becoming aware of new information and skills, and creating dissonance with a teacher's current position. These processes are not mutually exclusive: All may be present in a given professional learning opportunity." Perhaps more importantly, our understanding of the vignettes provides a way of seeing how professional learning opportunities can achieve the goals that are set for them. By this, we mean that rather than hoping that a professional learning opportunity will address teachers' learning needs, a number of factors can be taken into account in the planning stage. These factors can be posed as a series of questions. The first is this: Within a department, does the planning of professional learning opportunities take into account teachers' motivations for learning? In asking this question, we are really getting to the heart of why teachers should be involved in professional learning. The second question is about our intentionality: Are we being deliberate in giving teachers permission to question and experiment with the reform? If we are, then the chances of the reform becoming embedded in practice are greatly improved. In turn, this success provides a platform for subsequent reforms to be enacted. Remember: Reform is an itinerant process. Third, in our quest for teacher professional learning, are we paying attention to the teacher as a whole person? If we do not support teachers as they struggle with reform and, conversely, celebrate their successes, then we are missing the vital humanity that underpins all great teaching.

With that thought in mind, we reach the end of the vignettes, stories drawn together through years of experience in learning how to teach from a reformed perspective. From the issues that young teachers face in establishing themselves in our profession to late-career teachers clearly enthused by their work to chairs who are building departments that want to learn, there is much to be learned from each of our colleagues. We thank them all.

Summary

- Three learning processes are important for teachers' professional learning: "cueing and retrieving prior knowledge, becoming aware of new information and skills, and creating dissonance with a teacher's current position" (Timperley et al. 2007, p. 7).

- Our moral concern for students as teachers is a powerful motivation for change and is also key to sustaining the improvements to teaching and learning, especially when the work of reform is difficult.

- Although teachers are highly motivated to provide the best for their students, they also understand (better than anyone else) that "teaching is a difficult and nuanced act, and there needs to be a good reason, and a good chance of success, to change" (Julie).

- Learning comes with several conditions attached. To learn, there must be dissatisfaction with the current situation, what is being proposed must be intelligible, and the new ideas must be perceived as initially plausible.

- Schools and departments need to be well connected to a range of professional learning providers and opportunities—such as professional associations and their resources, conferences, and the expertise that exists in neighboring schools, local universities, and board or district initiatives—if they are to identify and leverage important professional learning resources that can support teacher learning.

Questions to Consider

1. Within a department, does the planning of professional learning opportunities take into account teachers' motivations for learning? If so, in what ways? If not, how might this be done in the future?

2. Are we (schools, departments, and teacher leaders) being deliberate in giving teachers permission to question and experiment with the reform? What strategies are in place for doing this?

3. In our quest for teacher professional learning, are we paying attention to the teacher as a whole person? Do we show empathy and support for teachers as they navigate real change, like that called for in the *NGSS*?

4. How can we connect to a range of professional learning providers and opportunities—such as professional associations and their resources, conferences, the expertise that exists in neighboring schools, local universities, and board or district initiatives—to support teachers' professional learning?

And Now the Work Begins ...

And so we reach the final chapter. In the last seven chapters, we have considered how science can be more accurately represented in the classroom, pondered a framework for building the science department, and seen how that framework has been experienced in the lives of a number of teachers. Throughout this work, we have tried to emphasize the balance that exists between theory and practice, for they really do inform one another and improve our teaching and learning. In this chapter, we want to draw out the main lessons that we have learned and how they may guide you in your work.

We know from research that teachers' careers do not follow a linear path. Huberman (1989, 1993), among others, has detailed how teachers move through a range of stages, from survival and discovery in the early years, to stabilization, experimentation, stocktaking, and diversification in the middle years, to serenity or conservatism and disengagement in the latter years. Knowledge of these career phases helps us make sense of our colleagues' professional learning experiences and adds a richness to our understanding of the framework that Timperley et al. (2007) propose for building effective professional learning that supports reforms such as the *A Framework for K–12 Science Education* (the *Framework*) and the *Next Generation Science Standards* (*NGSS*). This framework addresses the context and content of professional learning, the activities that promote professional learning, and the learning processes that teachers engage in. In Chapter 3, we explored each of these components and their constituent areas. In Chapter 4, we explored each component through the lived experiences of our colleagues. What our colleagues' vignettes make clear is that there are variations within the framework and its component areas, and it is from these variations that we can learn some important lessons. Those lessons include how the professional learning needs of teachers change over time, the centrality of teacher leaders in promoting teacher professional learning, and how it is the intangibles in the life of a department that can make the crucial difference between being open to or rejecting learning opportunities. We finish the chapter with some resources that may be of help as you work within your department.

Supporting the Changing Needs of Teachers

Throughout their careers, teachers are constantly learning, but the content, context, activities, and processes of that learning are constantly evolving. In the early years, this learning centers on establishing a teacher identity and everything that goes with that: how to teach, how students learn, the personal qualities that one needs to develop, and understanding the school and professional environment. Following these years, a period of stabilization involves making a commitment to the profession, a mastery of teaching and learning, and a greater emphasis on the needs of students. Building on these foundations, the middle years of teachers' careers tend to be marked by greater experimentation with teaching and learning, a diversification of teaching and learning strategies, and the acceptance of leadership roles (both formal and informal). This is also a period of stocktaking when teachers consider their careers and the possibility of career change. On the negative side, these middle years may also see an increasingly negative view of change and professional learning. The final phases of teachers' careers can last from their 19th year until retirement. A sense of serenity can include an acceptance of the professional self, a reinvigoration of teaching and learning, and an increasing realization of generational differences. In turn, this can lead to an increasing sense of conservatism, inflexibility, and discontent. Closer to retirement, teachers can also develop a disengagement from the profession—a state that can reflect the serene or bitter dispositions of the later years.

The vignettes make clear that supporting these changing needs of teachers is the responsibility of both the individual teacher and the department (and, by extension, the wider education community). Although there is no doubt that teachers need to be proactive in seeking out professional learning opportunities, the strategies for encouraging teachers will vary depending on the experience of the teacher. Early-career teachers need to know that there are individual teachers who can act as mentors. Although some jurisdictions have established mentorship programs, the key to success lies in establishing strong personal and professional relationships between teachers. These relationships allow knowledge about the teaching and learning of science to be shared, tested, and validated. Linking these mentoring relationships to professional associations, such as the National Science Teachers Association (NSTA), introduces beginning teachers to the wider education community and builds commitment. The vignettes also suggest that the professional learning of an early-career teacher benefits when there is a consistent message as to what the department values as "good" science teaching. This is an important point for leaders to note, for if the department holds a traditional view of science education, then that is what the beginning teacher will be socialized into. If the department is working to reform its practices, then communicate this to the beginning teacher and help him or her get involved.

For midcareer teachers to those approaching retirement, these same strong relationships need to be formed or maintained, but they serve as the context in which teachers can continue to take calculated risks to challenge and improve their teaching. An important catalyst to change is the continued engagement of teachers with the wider science education community. In each vignette, our colleagues were working with professional associations, reading science education research, and working with external expertise across a range of facets of their work. Engagement with the wider community is crucial, but in the end, professional learning for teachers—and the risks that learning entails—needs to happen in an environment in which it is understood that things can, and do, go wrong. In a department that understands this, teachers can work together, knowing that although they agree on the main focus of their reform efforts, they may not agree on everything, but they will be there to support each other. Only through working together can teachers reach the level of collaboration that supports a personal renaissance in teaching and learning and the passing on of reformed practices to new members of the department.

Although the vignettes highlight these changing professional learning needs of teachers, they also highlight four foundations for teacher professional learning within departments, regardless of the teachers' career stage. As summarized by Reiser (2013), teacher professional learning is always firmly grounded in the subject matter, is always active in sense making and problem solving, is always firmly connected to teacher practice, and is always supported in a coherent way. It is the role of teacher leaders in supporting learning that we turn to next.

The Role of the Teacher Leader

We use the term *teacher leader* loosely, referring both to those with formal leadership roles, such as chairs, and to those teachers who provide leadership within their department and often beyond. The key characteristic of teacher leaders, we believe, is that they are committed to developing a trusting environment in which their colleagues are free, and indeed encouraged, to challenge and improve the teaching and learning of science. Further, teacher leaders are proactive in developing professional learning opportunities for teachers to visit, and then revisit, how they conceptualize reforms to teaching and learning in light of their growing expertise.

The development of trusting environments is seen in each vignette. For each of our colleagues, there was an explicit trust in the work of their colleagues and in their department as a whole. This trust was reflected in the ways that our colleagues approached their work—always seeking to understand where the people they work with are in their professional lives, their understanding of teaching and learning, and their learning needs. It was also reflected in the work of the chairs (both Liz and Julie and the chairs of Shawn's and Mike and Steve's departments), who intentionally encouraged their departments to be actively involved with reform efforts and who accepted that learning involves risk. In each case, our colleagues understood the need to change, were given viable alternatives to work with, and worked in an environment where they could safely accept an increasing personal responsibility for reforming their practices. By involving teachers in the work of reform and the wider science education community, each department built a strong commitment to reform, even as they proceeded along different paths.

We can use the work of Peacock (2014) in understanding the qualities of teacher leadership that we see in the vignettes. Possession of the following capabilities allows leaders in science education to offer instructional leadership to their colleagues.

Science Leadership Content Knowledge

Leaders need to be credible, as this models what reformed instruction looks like. Credibility allows the leader to start influencing curriculum, instructional, and assessment decisions.

Advocating for Science and Science Education

Leaders need to be current with developments in science education, as this provides a benchmark and tools for the department to work with in the task of reform.

Building a Collegial Learning Environment

As the vignettes make clear, a collegial learning environment needs to focus on teachers' content and pedagogical knowledge and students' ways of learning. To do this, there must be active professional learning opportunities that are grounded in teachers' practices but that are also coherent with the goals of the *Framework* and the *NGSS*.

Negotiating Context and Solving Problems

More a role for chairs and the authority that comes with their position, there is always a need to be able to work with administrators to support the professional learning in their department. In negotiating the work of the department, a leader needs to make political decisions and have the power to carry them out. As we have seen in the vignettes, the chair who maintains a moral presence through his or her enunciation of clear values is more likely to be successful in this area.

This recognition of the importance of values leads us to the final lesson that we can draw from the vignettes: how intangibles in the life of a department can make the crucial difference between being open to or rejecting learning opportunities.

Intangibles

When teachers and administrators talk of professional learning, they often limit themselves to the materials and resources that are needed to meet some objective. What is often downplayed is the value that teachers place on being intrinsically motivated by and meaningfully engaged with professional learning that works to improve their practices. Each one of our colleagues wrote of their commitment to student success and of the power of relationships in shaping their own learning. When we talk of intangibles, we are talking of teachers' beliefs, emotions, and values, as well as their relationships to their colleagues, students, and workplace. If we ignore these factors, then we run the risk of reducing professional learning to a mechanistic exercise that may concentrate on knowledge acquisition to the detriment of the human aspects of education.

Looking back over the vignettes, a common thread runs throughout all four components of the Timperley et al. (2007) framework for professional learning. Regardless of experience, academic background, or formal leadership position within the department, each of our colleagues placed a significant value on the intangible aspects of their work. The context of professional learning was heavily shaped by the need for trusting relationships; the content of professional learning was heavily invested in understanding how students learn; the activities supporting professional learning were underpinned by talk of collaboration and community; and learning processes were predicated on supporting (both cognitively and emotionally) professional learning that was motivated by a strong desire for student success. What our colleagues are saying is crystal clear—if we are to build departments that support and encourage professional learning, we must tend to the people who are in our departments. This does not mean acquiescing to every whim or demand that is made to those who would seek to build the department. As Mike said, "we don't have to agree with all of it—the purpose is to generate self-reflection and then conversation." Building the department requires leadership that is "about helping people understand the problems they face, helping them manage these problems, and even helping them learn to live with them" (Sergiovanni 2005, p. 118). That is the real challenge, and it is never easy. But if a department is built on common understandings and values of what is important in science education and teachers are collaboratively engaged in questioning, challenging, and improving their practices against the ideals of reform documents, then we will be well on the way to providing a science education that benefits all students.

Where to Next?

In this book, we have considered a framework for considering teacher professional learning and have looked at how teachers at various stages of their careers work within that framework. We have seen how teachers' professional learning needs change over the course of their careers, how teacher leaders can shape professional learning opportunities within departments, and how we must never lose sight of the human dimension of our profession. The work of building the department has no fixed start date, and there is certainly no end date, as departments are dynamic places. We trust that the experiences of our colleagues and the ideas that we have distilled from them are of benefit to you in your work. The following resources contain a wealth of material aimed at many of the issues that we have raised here. We wish you well as you undertake the important work of building science departments that promote teacher professional learning, the ideals of science education found in documents such as the *Framework* and the *NGSS*, and, most important, high-quality teaching and learning for all students.

Please feel free to contact us if we can help you with anything.

Resources
For Administrators

1. *An overview for principals.* Available from *www.nextgenscience.org/sites/default/files/resource/files/NGSS%20Overview%20for%20Principals_0.pdf.*

2. Brunsell, E., D. M. Kneser, and K. J. Niemi. 2014. *Introducing teachers and administrators to the* NGSS: *A professional development facilitator's guide.* Arlington, VA: NSTA Press.

For Departments

1. Melville, W., D. Jones, and T. Campbell. 2015. *Reimagining the science department.* Arlington, VA: NSTA Press.

2. Wilson, S., H. Schweingruber, and H. Nielsen, eds. 2015. *Teachers' learning: Enhancing opportunities, creating supportive contexts.* Washington, DC: National Academies Press. Also available online at *www.nap.edu/catalog/21836/science-teachers-learning-enhancing-opportunities-creating-supportive-contexts.*

3. *Science professional learning standards.* Available from *www.csss-science.org/downloads/SPLS.pdf.*

4. Lee, O., E. Miller, and R. Januszyk. 2014. NGSS *for all students.* Arlington, VA: NSTA Press.

5. *NSTA position statement on professional development in science education.* Available from *www.nsta.org/about/positions/profdev.aspx.*

6. Reiser, B. 2013. What professional development strategies are needed for successful implementation of the *Next Generation Science Standards?* Available from *www.ets.org/Media/Research/pdf/reiser.pdf.*

7. Moulding, B., R. Bybee, and P. Paulson. 2015. *A vision and plan for science teaching and learning: An educator's guide to* A Framework for K–12 Science Education, Next Generation Science Standards, *and state science standards.* Salt Lake City: Essential Teaching and Learning Publications.

For Teachers

1. Achieve *NGSS.* Available from *www.nextgenscience.org.*

2. *NSTA position statement on induction programs for the support and development of beginning teachers of science.* Available from *www.nsta.org/about/positions/induction.aspx.*

3. NGSS@NSTA (resource hub). Available from *http://ngss.nsta.org.*

4. STEM teaching tools. Available from *http://stemteachingtools.org.*

5. Tools for ambitious science teaching. Available from *http://ambitiousscienceteaching.org.*

Summary

- Throughout their careers, teachers are constantly learning. Similarly, the content, context, activities, and processes of that learning constantly evolve. For early-career teachers, the key to success lies in establishing strong personal and professional relationships between teachers. These relationships allow knowledge about the teaching and learning of science to be shared, tested, and validated. For midcareer teachers to those approaching retirement, these same strong relationships need to be formed or maintained, but they serve as the context in which teachers can continue to take calculated risks to challenge and improve their teaching.

- Only through working together can teachers reach the level of collaboration that supports a personal renaissance in teaching and learning and the passing on of reformed practices to new members of the department.

- Teacher professional learning is always firmly grounded in the subject matter, is always active in sense making and problem solving, is always firmly connected to teacher practice, and is always supported in a coherent way.

- The key characteristic of teacher leaders, we believe, is that they are committed to developing a trusting environment in which their colleagues are free, and indeed encouraged, to challenge and improve the teaching and learning of science. Further, teacher leaders are proactive in developing professional learning opportunities for teachers to visit, and then revisit, how they conceptualize reforms to teaching and learning in light of their growing expertise.

- Intangibles are teachers' beliefs, emotions, and values, as well as their relationships to their colleagues, students, and workplace. If we ignore these factors, then we run the risk of reducing professional learning to a mechanistic exercise that may concentrate on knowledge acquisition to the detriment of the human aspects of education.

- If a department is built on common understandings and values of what is important in science education and teachers are collaboratively engaged in questioning, challenging, and improving their practices against the ideals of reform documents, then the department will be well on the way to providing a science education that benefits all students.

Questions to Consider

1. What are ways you can envision meeting the differing needs of teachers at different stages of their careers within the department?

2. What are ways in which relationships are forged with new department members, and how are new members of the department brought into conversations about the commitments of the science department related to science teaching and learning?

3. What are ways in which you can recognize the coherency of your department's support for professional learning? What are ways current support for professional learning could be made even more coherent?

4. Intangibles are teachers' beliefs, emotions, and values, as well as their relationships to their colleagues, students, and workplace. In what ways can the department support teachers' navigation of these intangibles in ways that are more likely to lead to continued professional learning for teachers?

5. Can your department describe its common understandings and values related to what is important in science education? If so, would all in the department articulate these similarly? If not, what are ways to begin to elicit and agree on common understandings and values related to what is important in science education?

References

Aikenhead, G. 2006. *Science education for everyday life.* New York: Teachers College Press.

Baker, W. P., M. Lang, and A. E. Lawson. 2002. Classroom management for successful student inquiry. *Classroom Management* 75 (5): 248–252.

Banilower, E., P. S. Smith, I. Weiss, K. Malzahn, K. Campbell, and A. Weis. 2013. *Report of the 2012 national survey of science and mathematics education.* Chapel Hill, NC: Horizon Research.

Berman, P., and M. W. McLaughlin. 1978. *Federal programs supporting educational change: Implementing and sustaining innovations.* Santa Monica, CA: Rand Corporation.

Blenkin, G. M., G. Edwards, and A. V. Kelly. 1997. Perspectives on educational change. In *Organizational effectiveness and improvement in education,* ed. A. Harris, N. Bennett, and M. Preedy, 216–230. Buckingham, UK: Open University Press.

Brundrett, M., and I. Terrell. 2004. *Learning to lead in the secondary school: Becoming an effective head of department.* London: Routledge Falmer.

Bybee, R. 2011. Scientific and engineering practices in K–12 classrooms: Understanding a framework for K–12 science education. *The Science Teacher* 78 (9): 34–40.

Bybee, R. W. 2015. *The BSCS 5E Instructional Model: Creating teachable moments.* Arlington, VA: NSTA Press.

Campbell, T., C. Schwarz, and M. Windschitl. 2016. What we call misconceptions may be necessary stepping-stones on a path towards making sense of the world. *The Science Teacher* 83 (3): 69–74.

Carlone, H. B. 2003. Innovative science within and against a culture of "achievement." *Science Education* 87 (3): 307–328.

Cochran-Smith, M., and S. L. Lytle. 1999. Relationships of knowledge and practice: Teacher learning in communities. In *Review of research in education,* 24, ed. A. Iran-Nejad and P. D. Pearson, 249–305. Washington, DC: American Educational Research Association.

Collins, J. 2001. *Good to great: Why some companies make the leap … and others don't.* New York: HarperCollins.

Dana, N. F., and D. Yendol-Silva. 2003. *The reflective educator's guide to classroom research: Learning to teach and teaching to learn through practitioner inquiry.* Thousand Oaks, CA: Corwin Press.

Darling-Hammond, L. 2001. Constructing 21st-century teacher education. *Journal of Teacher Education* 57 (3): 300–314.

Darling-Hammond, L., and G. Sykes, eds. 1999. *Teaching as the learning profession: Handbook of policy and practice.* San Francisco: Jossey-Bass.

Ely, D. P. 1990. Conditions that facilitate the implementation of educational technology innovations. *Journal of Research on Computing in Education* 23 (2): 298–305.

Feiman-Nemser, S. 1990. Teacher preparation: Structural and conceptual alternatives. In *Handbook of research on teacher education,* ed. W. R. Houston, 212–233. New York: Macmillan.

Fielding, M., S. Bragg, J. Craig, I. Cunningham, M. Eraut, S. Gillinson, M. Horne, C. Robinson, and

References

J. Thorp. 2005. *Factors influencing the transfer of good practice*. Research Report RR615, Department for Education and Skills, University of Sussex, Brighton, UK.

Ford, M. 2008. "Grasp of practice" as a reasoning resource for inquiry and nature of science understanding. *Science & Education* 17 (2): 147–177.

Fullan, M. 1992. *What's worth fighting for?* Buckingham, UK: Open University Press.

Garet, M. S., A. C. Porter, L. Desimone, B. F. Birman, and K. S. Yoon. 2001. What makes professional learning effective? Results from a national sample of teachers. *American Educational Research Journal* 38 (4): 915–945.

Giere, R. 2004. How models are used to represent reality. *Philosophy of Science* 71 (5): 742–752.

Goodrum, D., M. Hackling, and L. Rennie. 2001. *The status and quality of teaching and learning of science in Australian schools*. Canberra, ACT: Department of Education, Training and Youth Affairs.

Goodson, I. F. 1993. *School subjects and curriculum change*. 3rd. ed. London: Falmer Press.

Hargreaves, D. H. 2000. The knowledge creating school. In *Leading professional development in education*, ed. B. Moon, J. Butcher, and E. Bird, 224–240. London: Routledge Falmer.

Harris, K., F. Jensz, and G. Baldwin. 2005. *Who's teaching science? Meeting the demand for qualified science teachers in Australian secondary schools*. Waurn Ponds VIC 3216, Australia: The Australian Council of Deans of Science.

Havelock, R. G., and S. Zlotolow. 1995. *The change agent's guide*. Englewood Cliffs, NJ: Educational Technology.

Henderson, J. B., A. MacPherson, J. Osborne, and A. Wild. 2015. Beyond construction: Five arguments for the role and value of critique in learning science. *International Journal of Science Education* 37 (10): 1668–1697.

Hodson, D. 2003. Time for action: Science education for an alternative future. *International Journal of Science Education* 25 (6): 645–670.

Hodson, D. 2011. *Looking towards the future*. Rotterdam, Netherlands: Sense Publishers.

Hord, S. M. 1997. Professional learning communities: What are they and why are they important? *Issues … About Change* 6 (1). *www.sedl.org/change/issues/issues61.html*

Huberman, M. A. 1989. The professional life cycle of teachers. *Teachers College Record* 91 (1): 31–57.

Huberman, M. A. 1992. Teacher development and instructional mastery. In *Understanding teacher development*, ed. A. Hargreaves and M. Fullan, 122–142. New York: Teachers College Press.

Huberman, M. A. 1993. *The lives of teachers*. New York: Teachers College Press.

Judson, E., and A. E. Lawson. 2007. What is the role of constructivist teachers within faculty communication networks? *Journal of Research in Science Teaching* 44 (3): 490–505.

Krajcik, J. 2015. Three-dimensional instruction: Using a new type of teaching in the science classroom. *The Science Teacher* 83 (8): 50–52.

Latour, B. 2004. Why has critique run out of steam? From matters of fact to matters of concern. *Critical Inquiry* 30 (2): 225–248.

Layton, D. 1981. The schooling of science in England, 1854–1939. In *The parliament of science*, ed. R. MacLeod and P. Collins, 188–210. Northwood, UK: Science Reviews Ltd.

Luria, A. R. 1976. *Cognitive development*. Cambridge, MA: Harvard University Press.

Melville, W., and J. Wallace. 2007. Metaphorical duality: High school subject departments as both communities and organizations. *Teaching and Teacher Education* 23 (7): 1193–1205.

Mundry, S. 2005. Changing perspectives in professional development. *The Science Educator* 14 (1): 9–15.

National Research Council (NRC). 1996. *National Science Education Standards.* Washington, DC: National Academies Press.

National Research Council (NRC). 2012. *A framework for K–12 science education: Practices, crosscutting concepts, and core ideas.* Washington, DC: National Academies Press.

National Research Council (NRC). 2015. *Science teachers' learning: Enhancing opportunities, creating supportive contexts.* Washington, DC: National Academies Press.

Nersessian, N. J. 1999. Model-based reasoning in conceptual change. In *Model-based reasoning in scientific discovery,* ed. L. Magnani, N. J. Nersessian, and P. Thagard, 5–22. New York: Kluwer Academic/Plenum Press.

NGSS Lead States. 2013. *Next Generation Science Standards: For states, by states.* Washington, DC: National Academies Press.

Osborne, J. 2010. Arguing to learn in science: The role of collaborative, critical discourse. *Science* 328 (23): 463–466.

Pashler, H., M. McDaniel, D. Rohrer, and R. Bjork. 2008. Learning styles: Concepts and evidence. *Psychological Science in the Public Interest* 9 (3): 106–119.

Peacock, J. S. 2014. Science instructional leadership: The role of the department chair. *Science Educator* 23 (1): 36–48.

Posner, G. J., K. A. Strike, P. W. Hewson, and W. A. Gertzog. 1982. Accommodation of a scientific conception: Towards a theory of conceptual change. *Science Education* 66 (2): 211–227.

Reiser, B. J. 2013. What professional development strategies are needed for successful implementation of the Next Generation Science Standards? Paper presented at the Invitational Research Symposium on Science Assessment, September 24–25, Washington, DC. *www.ets.org/research/policy_research_reports/publications/paper/2013/jvgw.*

Rennie, L. J. 2010. *Evaluation of the Science by Doing Stage One professional learning approach 2010.* Canberra, Australia: Australian Academy of Science.

Riley, K. 2000. Leadership, learning and systemic reform. *The Journal of Educational Change* 1 (1): 29–55.

Sergiovanni, T. J. 2005. The virtues of leadership. *The Educational Forum* 69 (2): 112–123.

Sheppard, K., and D. M. Robbins. 2007. High school biology today: What the Committee of Ten actually said. *Life Sciences Education* 6 (3): 198–202.

Stroupe, D., and M. Windschitl. 2015. Supporting ambitious instruction by beginning teachers with specialized tools and practices. In *Newly hired teachers of science: A better beginning,* ed. J. Luft and S. Dubois, 181–196. Rotterdam, Netherlands: Sense Publishers.

Teacher Training Agency. 1998. *National standards for subject leaders.* London: Her Majesty's Stationery Office.

Timperley, H., A. Wilson, H. Barrar, and I. Fung. 2007. *Teacher professional learning and development.* Wellington, New Zealand: Ministry of Education. *www.oecd.org/edu/school/48727127.pdf.*

Tytler, R. 2007. *Re-imagining science education: Engaging students in science for Australia's future.* Camberwell, Victoria, Australia: Australian Council for Educational Research.

Vygotsky, L. S. 1978. *Mind and society: The development of higher mental processes.* Cambridge, MA: Harvard University Press.

Vygotsky, L. S. 1987 [1934]. Thinking and speech. In *Collected works* (Vol. 1), ed. R. Rieber and A. Carton and trans. N. Minick, 39–285. New York: Plenum.

Welch, W. W., L. E. Klopfer, G. S. Aitkenhead, and J. T. Robinson. 1981. The role of inquiry in science education: Analysis and recommendations. *Science Education* 65 (1): 33–50.

References

White, R. T. 1988. *Learning science.* Oxford: Basil Blackwell.

Wildy, H., and J. Wallace. 2004. Science as content, science as context: Working in the science department. *Research in Science Education* 30 (2): 99–112.

Wilson, S., and Berne, J. 1999. Teacher learning and the acquisition of professional knowledge: An examination of research on contemporary professional development. *Review of Research in Education* 24: 173–209.

Yager, R. E. 2005. Achieving the staff development model advocated in the national standards. *The Science Educator* 14 (1): 16–24.

Appendix
The Components of Professional Learning and Their Constituent Areas

(From Timperley et al. 2007)

The Professional Learning Context

1. Infrastructural Supports

   These include funding and/or teacher release time for professional learning. The studies that were analyzed did not provide conclusive evidence as to the impact of these supports on teacher professional learning.

2. Coherence With Policy

   In this area, approaches to science teaching are promoted that are consistent with both current research findings and their policy contexts. This is an important consideration, for "all cases of professional development that led to positive outcomes for students were part of wider and coherent movements in science teaching and learning that were underpinned by strong research bases" (Timperley et al. 2007, p. 105).

3. Voluntary or Compulsory Involvement

   Volunteering was not a necessary condition for successful professional development, but neither was it a guarantee of change. The content and form of the professional learning opportunities were more important than volunteering in achieving teacher buy-in.

4. Independent or Collaborative

   A similar proportion of studies involved teachers participating in professional development independently of their school colleagues and teachers participating as part of a whole science department. Core studies in which teachers participated independently of their school colleagues developed collegial groups among participants.

5. External Expertise

All of the core studies involved expertise from outside the participants' school environments. "Cascading" models of professional development, in which external providers trained teachers as trainers had mixed outcomes but could be successful under certain circumstances.

6. School Leadership

Insufficient information was provided to draw conclusions about school leaders' involvement. Departmental leadership has been shown to have a positive impact on developing opportunities for professional learning.

7. Time and Frequency

All of the core studies involved professional development over extended periods of at least one school year, with some up to five years, with relatively frequent input, particularly in the initial stages. One-off learning opportunities may be sufficient to bring about changes that are of limited scope, but not substantive changes in practice and outcomes.

8. Prevailing Discourses

Some cases of professional development were successful despite initial differences between the prevailing discourses of the teachers and the ideas being promoted. This point is particularly important in terms of the cultural issues teachers face in changing their attitudes toward science and teaching practices.

9. Professional Learning Goals

In all of the interventions in the core studies, professional learning goals specific to science were explicitly shared with teachers.

The Content of Professional Learning

1. Content to Support a Particular Program

   Opportunities for professional learning often provided detailed science content related to particular instructional programs.

2. Integration of Theory and Practice

   All of the core studies developed theoretical understandings that went beyond immediate practice.

3. Pedagogical Content Knowledge

   In most cases that were studied, teachers' science content knowledge developed, but teachers often regarded the process of learning as more important than the content knowledge itself. In all cases, the development of content knowledge also developed teachers' pedagogical knowledge.

4. Knowledge of Assessment

   For teachers, improving assessment was closely related to learning science content, although a change in emphasis on students' conceptual understanding required changes in assessment practices.

The Activities That Promote Professional Learning

1. Sequencing of Activities

   Effective professional learning initially involves some direct teaching of a new concept, which is then followed by a range of activities designed to support the transfer of the concept into practice.

2. Activities to Translate Theory Into Practice

   In all of the studies, participants were provided with at least two different types of professional learning activities, but no particular type was universal.

3. Demonstrations of Classroom Practice

   The studies make explicit the need to provide teachers with opportunities to see particular approaches implemented in real or simulated classroom situations.

4. Receiving Instructional Materials

   The majority of the studies provided teachers with substantial support in the form of instructional materials, but these were never regarded as sufficient by themselves.

5. Being Observed and Receiving Feedback

   Interestingly, most of the core studies did not provide opportunities for teachers to be observed and receive feedback in their classrooms.

6. Teachers Taking Part in Learning Activities Positioned as Students

   Reported in only two studies, this activity appears to be useful in some circumstances but generally has limited effectiveness.

7. Comparing Teachers' Own Theories With New Theories

   In three studies, teachers were actively engaged in comparing their beliefs about teaching and learning with new conceptualizations of knowledge. This work resulted in teachers having considerable input into the reform of their practices.

8. Participating in Professional Communities

   All of the core studies involved teachers participating in some form of learning community in which they shared their ideas, experiences, and challenges to support each other to implement changed practices.

The Learning Processes That Teachers Engage In

1. New Information

   The synthesis highlighted the crucial role of information that deepened understandings and refined the skills needed by teachers to be consistent with the new practices demanded of them.

2. Creating Dissonance With Current Position (Values and Beliefs)

   Only two core studies explicitly reported the creation of dissonance, but the difference between traditional approaches to science and those advocated in the professional development indicates that dissonance was likely to have been a common feature.

3. Consolidating Prior Knowledge

   Cueing, retrieving, and consolidating prior knowledge were explicitly reported in only two studies.

Index

Page numbers printed in **boldface type** indicate figures.

A

Activities, sequencing of, 33, 34
Activity theory, 2, **2**
 objects, 2, 3, 4
 subjects, 2, 3
 tools, 2, 3
Aikenhead, G., 14
Ambitious Science Teaching, 9
American Association for the Advancement of
 Science, 12
Assessment, 31, 32–33, 66–68, 68–69, 90,
 111–112
 colleagues leading on, 68–69, 74–75
 and evaluation, focus on, 66–68
 knowledge of, 31, 32–33
Association for Science Education in the United
 Kingdom, 35

B

Biological Sciences Curriculum Study (BSCS),
 92
British Association for the Advancement of
 Science (BAAS), 12
British Teacher Training Agency, 20
Brundrett, M., and I. Terrell, 18

C

Career path of teachers, 123, 124–125
Change
 conditions that promote, 47
 in the department, 11–23
Churchill, Winston, 46
Classroom
 experiences, current *vs. NGSS*, 4–5
 practice demonstrations, 33, 34

Cochran-Smith, M., and S. L. Lytle, 20
Collaboration, 51
 time, 49
Colleagues
 learning from, 84–85
 planning with, 89–90
 support, 25, 26
Collegiality, 41, 45
 collegial learning environment, building, 126
Collins, Jim, 47
Committee of Ten, 12
Community, 87, 97–100
Conditions for learning within departments,
 25–38
 colleague support, 25, 26
 control of professional learning, 26
 framework for professional learning, 27–28
 insights and practices, develop, 25
 integration of evolving beliefs into teaching
 practices, 25
 lecturing, 25
 questioning practices, 25
 shared knowledge about engaging students,
 develop, 25
 shared knowledge base for issues of student
 learning, 26
Conformity to traditional view of science, 16
Constructivism in science education, 13
Content. *See* Professional learning content
CREATER change model, 92–94
Crosscutting concepts, 3, 17, 29
 Cause and Effect, 4
 Energy and Matter, 3
 Systems and System Models, 4
Cultural issues, 11, 12–15, 21

D

Darling-Hammond, L., 29, 92
Darwin, 2–3
Department. *See also* Conditions for learning within departments; Leadership in the department; Science department, importance of
    change, 11–23
    conditions for learning in, 25–38
    leadership, 11, 19–21
    meetings, 48–49, 53
    structures, 40, 47
Disciplinary core ideas, 17, 29
    Matter and Its Interactions, 3

E

Ely, D. P., 47
Evaluation, 66–68
Experimentation by teachers, 124
Expertise
    external, 28, 30
    mix of internal and external, 16
"Explaining the Outbreak of Lyme Disease in the Middle School Life Science Classroom," 7–8
Explain phenomena or solve problems, 3

F

Facts in science teaching, 26
Feedback, 33, 34–35
Fielding, M. et al, 19
A Framework for K–12 Science Education, 1, 3, 9, 14, 15, 16, 18, 19, 20, 25, 26, 28, 29, 32, 33, 36, 61, 64, 65, 73, 97, 108, 123
Fullan, M., 52, 101

G

Giere, R., 2
Goodrum D., M. Hackling, and L. Rennie, 51
Good to Great: Why Some Companies Make the Leap ... and Others Don't (Collins), 47

H

Havelock, R. G., and S. Zlotolow, 92
Hierarchy of school science subjects, 12–13
Hodson, D., 13
Huberman, M. A., 34, 56, 123

I

Intangibles, 127
Integration of theory and practice, 31, 32

K

Koch, Robert, 13

L

Latour, B., 13
Leadership in the department, 11, 19–21
Learning, collaborative, 20
"Learning About Forces and Motion With Ramps in the Middle School Life Science Classroom," 6
Learning processes teachers engage in, 27, 105–121
    "Again, That's Science," 112–113
    "And Yes, I Am Guilty of That, Too," 106–108
    assessment, 111–112
    "Breaking Down What I Knew," 111–112
    change in a system, 113–115
    credibility of reform, 117
    deliberateness, 117–118
    direct observations, 107–108
    dissonance between what teachers are doing and what they should be doing, 110–111
    "How Can We Investigate Change?," 113–115
    learning from students, 106–107
    motivation, 115–116
    and *NGSS,* 108–110
    reformed teaching, 112–113
    support for learning processes, 118–119
    "There Became Some Natural Dissonance," 108–111
Learning styles, 69
Lecturing, 25
Ledru-Rollin, Alexandre, 100

M

Materials, instructional, 33, 34
    receiving, 33, 34
Motivation, 115–116

N

National Research Council, 28, 48

National Science Education Standards (NRC), 9, 48, 49
National Science Teachers Association (NSTA), 16, 30, 33, 97, 124
Nersession, N. J., 2
Next Generation Science Standards (*NGSS*), 1, 9, 14, 15, 16, 18, 19, 20, 25, 26, 28, 29, 32, 33, 36, 43, 44, 48, 51, 52, 56, 57, 61, 64, 65, 73, 74, 76, 78, 86, 87, 88, 97, 98, 101, 108–110, 116, 123
    becoming more familiar with, 87–88
NSTA Reports, 55

O
Objects, in activity theory, 2, 3, 4
Ontario Ministry of Education, 66, 68

P
Pasteur, Louis, 13
Peacock, J. S., 126
Pedagogy, building, 85
Physics First model, 65, 74, 78
Planning time, collaborative, 42–43
Policy
    coherence with, 28, 29
    documents, coherence with, 28
Political issues, 14
Position Statement on Professional Development in Science Education (NSTA), 16, 27, 33
Professional communities, participating in, 33, 35
Professionalization, 11, 12–15, 21
    allegiance to teaching facts, 14–15
    and disciplinary nature of science, 12
    hierarchy of school science subjects, 12–13
    and political issues, 14
    pure science *vs.* technological application, 12
    push for authentically representative scientific activity, 13
    resilience, 13
    soft science, 13
Professional learning, 11, 15–17, 21
    activities promoting professional learning, 27
    aim, long-term, 16–17
    collegial and collaborative learning, 16
    commitment to, 17
    control of, 26

    expertise, external, 28, 30
    expertise, mix of internal and external, 16
    framework for, 27–28
    goals, 28, 29
    investigation and inquiry, 16
    involvement, voluntary or compulsory, 28, 30
    leadership, 17
    learning activities, 16
    learning processes teachers engage in, 27
    planning, long-term coherent, 16
    policy, coherence with, 28, 29
    policy documents, coherence with, 28
    prevailing discourses, 28, 29
    purpose, sense of, 17
    questions, asking, 16
    reformation practices, 29
    school leadership, 28, 30
    science and teaching knowledge, integration of, 16
    and scientific activity, 15
    supports, infrastructural, 28, 30
    theory and practice, integration of, 16
    time and frequency, 28, 29
    value of, questioning, 15
    willingness to challenge individual and shared teaching beliefs, 17
Professional learning, activities promoting, 33–35, 83–94
    activities to translate theory into practice, 33, 34
    collaboration, 95–97
    colleagues, learning from, 84–85
    colleagues, planning with, 89–90
    community, 97–100
    community, considering, 87
    comparing own theories with new theories, 33, 35
    demonstrations of classroom practice, 33, 34
    district-coherent professional learning, 86–87
    grounding work with students, 91–92
    "I Can Foster Knowledge, Inquiry, and Creativity," 84–86
    information, 100–102
    instructional materials, receiving, 33, 34
    instructional rounds and common assessments, 90

interest of teachers, piquing, 92–93
learning from others, 85–86
NGSS, becoming more familiar with, 87–88
observation and receiving feedback, 33,
   34–35
pedagogy, building, 85
professional communities, 33, 35
professional readings, engaging with, 33, 35
sequencing of activities, 33, 34
support for teachers to dig deeper, 93–94
"They Are Teaching Me," 88–90
"We See Opportunities to Grow
   Professionally," 92–94
"We Started Moving Away From Direct
   Instruction," 86–88
work of others, supported by, 89
Professional learning communities, 46, 113–114
Professional learning content, 27, 30–33, 61–81
   "An Appreciation of Both Real Science *and*
      Real Teaching," 69–71
   assessment, colleagues leading on, 68–69,
      74–75
   assessment, knowledge of, 31, 32–33
   assessment and evaluation, focus on, 66–68
   classroom implementation, 71
   content, importance of, 70–71
   content to support a particular program, 31, 33
   disciplinary knowledge, broader and deeper,
      72–75
   disciplinary knowledge of science, 62
   engagement, modeling authentic, 64–65
   "Experience the Material," 64–65
   "I'm a Bit of a Dinosaur, But I've Learned,"
      68–69
   integration of theory and practice, 31, 32
   needs of those involved, 69–70
   past experiences, using, 65
   pedagogical content knowledge, 31, 32
   preparation requirements, 30–31
   reform as content, 66
   student learning methods, 78–79
   student learning methods, considering, 62–63
   "A 'Student of Science and of Education,'"
      62–63
   theory and practice, 76–78

"This Looks Very Different for Me Today,"
   66–68
Professional learning context, 27, 28–30, 39–59
   administrative support and reputation, 45
   "Building a Team of Science Teachers," 42–44
   chair's challenge, taking up, 46
   collaboration, 51
   collaboration time, 49
   collaborative planning time, 42–43
   collaborative structures, 43–44
   collegiality, 41, 45
   data-directed learning, 48
   departmental structures, 40, 47
   department meetings, 48–49, 53
   financial resources, 40
   "Is This Guy for Real?," 39–42
   "Modify It and Risk It All Again," 46
   professional learning community, 46
   reforms, 51
   relationships and trust, building, 48
   "The Right People on the Bus," 47–49
   school learning, beyond, 41–42
   support of administrators, 55–57
   time, 50–52
   trust, 52–55
   "We're Talking About How Science Is Done,"
      44–45
Professional learning processes, 35–36
   dissonance with current position, creating, 35,
      36
   new information, 35, 36
   prior knowledge, consolidating, 35, 36
Professional readings, 33, 35, 101
Public understanding of science, 14

R
Reform
   as content, 66
   credibility of, 117
   reformation practices, 29
   reformed teaching, 112–113
Reimagining the Science Department (NSTA),
   9, 97
Reiser, B. J., 31, 34, 61, 125
Resilience, 13
Resources

for administrators, 128
for departments, 128–129
for teachers, 129
Resources, financial, 40
Riley, K., 19

S
Science
education, debate over purposes of, 1
and engineering practices, 17
as inquiry, 25
pure *vs.* technological application, 12
soft, 13
Science department, importance of, 17–19, 21, 80
as communities, 17
constructivist approach, 18
influence over teaching and learning of teachers, 17–18
as organizations, 17
traditional approach, 18
Science leadership content knowledge, 126–127
advocating for science and science education, 126
collegial learning environment, building, 126
negotiating context and solving problems, 126
Science Teachers' Association of Ontario, 41
Science Teachers' Learning: Enhancing Opportunities, Creating Supportive Contexts (National Research Council), 28
Scientific activity, 1–10, **5**
classroom representations of, **5**
creating classroom environment to represent, 15
defined, 1
and department leadership, 19
and modeling, 2
and *NGSS,* 3–4
push for in classrooms, 13
understanding of how to represent in classroom, 19
Scientific Education in Schools (British Association for the Advancement of Science), 12
Scientific inquiry, 46
Sense making, 4

Student
engaging in science and engineering practices, 3
learning from, 106–107
learning methods, 78–79
learning methods, considering, 62–63
Subjects, in activity theory, 2, 3
Supports, infrastructural, 28, 30

T
Teacher
career path, 123, 124–125
experimentation, 124
interest of teachers, piquing, 92–93
leader, role of, 125–126
needs, supporting, 124–125
views of science, 18
Theories, comparison of, 33, 35
Theory and practice, 76–78
integration of, 16, 62–63
integration of theory and practice, 31, 32
Three-dimensional learning, 3, 4
example, 3
goals, 29
Timperley, H.A. et al, 21, 27, 33, 39, 79, 94, 105, 115, 119, 123, 127
Tools, in activity theory, 2, 3
Traditional view of science, conformity to, 16
Tytler, R., 13, 14

V
Values, struggles about, 11
Vignettes
"Explaining the Outbreak of Lyme Disease in the Middle School Life Science Classroom," 7–8
"Learning About Forces and Motion With Ramps in the Middle School Life Science Classroom," 6

W
Whewell, William, 12
Wildy, H., and J. Wallace, 18
Wilson, S., and J. Wallace, 25